The Cardinal

W9-AHB-437

NUMBER TWENTY-ONE
THE CORRIE HERRING HOOKS SERIES

JUNE OSBORNE

The Cardinal

PHOTOGRAPHS BY
BARBARA GARLAND

UNIVERSITY OF TEXAS PRESS
AUSTIN

LIBRARY OF CONGRESS
CATALOGING-IN-PUBLICATION DATA

Osborne, June, date.
    The cardinal / by June Osborne ; photographs by Barbara
Garland.—1st ed.
      p. cm.—(The Corrie Herring Hooks series ; no. 21)
Includes bibliographical references.
    ISBN 0-292-71147-6 (alk. paper)
    ISBN 0-292-76043-4 (pbk.)
    1. Cardinal-birds. I. Title. II. Series.
QL696.P2438O73   1992
598.8'83—dc20   91-48057

In the cardinal we have a rare combination of good qualities: brilliant plumage, a rich and pleasing voice, beneficial food habits, and devotion to its mate and family. Many of our best singers are not clothed in brilliant plumage, and many of our handsomest birds are not gifted musicians.

—Arthur Cleveland Bent,
Life Histories of North American Cardinals, Grosbeaks, Buntings, Towhees, Finches, Sparrows, and Allies

The female cardinal is soft grayish brown on the back,
with tinges of red on crest, tail, and wings.

Contents

Author's Acknowledgments
ix

Photographer's Acknowledgments
xi

Preface
xiii

Introduction
I

PART I   SEASONS IN THE LIFE OF THE CARDINAL
II

January:
Establishing Territory
13

February and March:
Winter Feeding, Range Expansion, and Courtship
23

April through July:
Nesting and Breeding Season
45

August and September:
Molting and Maintaining Feathers
77

October through December:
When Birds of a Feather Flock Together
87

PART 2   THE CARDINAL IN AMERICAN CULTURE
93

The Cardinal as Icon
95

The Cardinal at Christmas
101

Bibliography
105

In richness of plumage, elegance of motion, and strength of song, this species surpasses all its kindred in the United States.

—John James Audubon

Author's Acknowledgments

W hen I was first asked to write a book on the Northern Cardinal, my answer was a resounding yes. I responded affirmatively, first, because I admire this beautiful red bird. I am drawn to it in an aesthetic sense because of its splashy color and its clear, whistled notes that have cheered my days, as a Christmas card verse goes, "in the dark of December." Second, I said yes because I have observed this bird not only through my own "bird windows" on countless occasions, but also in almost every state and province within its range north of the Rio Grande, and in parts of Mexico as well. I have tromped through its preferred habitat on more occasions than I care to admit.

I knew I could not accomplish this assignment alone. Because stunning photographs should be a part of such a book to enhance the text and to catch the eye of the reader, I chose Barbara Garland to be the photographer to illustrate this work. I shall be eternally grateful for her tireless efforts and her willingness to take one more photograph—no matter how hot the Texas sun—to illustrate a certain point. There is no telling how many rolls of film she exposed to get the collection of pictures you now hold in your hands.

Nature writers, researchers, bird-watchers, and ornithologists through the ages unknowingly contributed to this book through the storehouse of knowledge gathered in professional journals, books, magazine articles, and occasional papers. Janet Sheets, reference librarian at Baylor University's Moody Library in Waco proved to be expert in retrieving these documents. Many thanks to her and all her assistants.

I owe an enormous debt of gratitude to Baylor University biology professor Frederick R. Gehlbach, who so generously allowed me to use his unpublished notes, which were the result of twenty years of intensive research and observation of the Northern Cardinal in Waco. Additionally, I thank him for reading the manuscript in one of its earliest forms and for his many suggestions and words of encouragement along the way.

Thanks to Brian K. Loflin, my friend and business partner, for the range map, and to Sam, my son, for the other drawings.

I think almost all my friends and acquaintances had a cardinal story to tell. I drew from many of those stories in writing this book, especially from the experiences of Floyce Moon's first-graders. And to all those who opened their homes and property to Barbara and to me that we could observe (or photograph) a certain cardinal behavior—thanks to you all.

I am grateful to Mary Jane Camp for providing the Hawaiian expression for *cheer,* and to Nathan Stone for the many trans-Pacific phone calls it took to get from her (his Aunty Mele) just the right word with the appropriate number of syllables to fit the cardinal's most familiar song.

I would be remiss if I did not acknowledge the undying patience and understanding of my husband, Harold, throughout the almost two years I was absorbed in completing this project. I thank him for reading and rereading the manuscript and for giving constructive criticism that kept me on track.

The most difficult task I faced during the entire process was to keep from attributing anthropomorphic characteristics to this best-loved bird. It is hard not to attribute human characteristics to a bird that is loved by so many. So, my apologies to any reader who is offended by my occasional slip-ups.

Finally, Barbara and I hope that this combination of pen and camera has produced a work both informative and beautiful—one that will be enjoyed by people of all ages for a long time to come.

Photographer's Acknowledgments

*T*o document the life history of the Northern Cardinal with pictures was a challenging assignment. Countless hours were spent sitting in a blind with the temperatures sometimes soaring. At other times the mercury plummeted.

In nature photography long hours of work do not always mean success. Some days I did not trip the shutter on my camera a single time. Other days, everything came together exactly right, and I exposed frame after frame of the beautiful cardinal.

During my ten years as a nature photographer, some of my most memorable shots have been taken as the direct result of a friend's help. This was also the case as I worked on *The Cardinal*. Many friends helped me in numerous ways. Billie Sue Mullen offered constructive suggestions regarding the project,

With his crimson plumage, the male cardinal is a striking subject to photograph.

for which I am deeply grateful. I also thank her for the countless ways she helped free my time for photography. Locating nests to photograph was a time-consuming activity. The following people helped: Bobbie Holland, Billy Lou Harper, John and Lavitha Dudley, Hollis Atkinson, Robert and Debbie Orr, and Leo and Sandra Dennis. Pam Moes made her backyard available to me on several occasions. Helen Hubler gave me access to her cardinal-rich farm and helped me construct a special bird feeder for photography, and John and Barbara Ingram made possible several shots on their property. Nell Smallwood and Mary Lee Bryan allowed me to erect a photo blind in their backyard, kept the feeder filled with sunflower seeds, and diligently reported cardinal activity to me.

June and I wish to thank Calvin Smith, Director of Baylor University's Strecker Museum in Waco, who graciously allowed us access to a museum specimen of a cardinal for the purpose of photographing the feathers to use as endpapers. We greatly appreciate this contribution and the assistance of his staff.

I thank Jim Mosley and Joe Irwin at Tom Padgitt, Inc., for technical assistance, and Tommie Suits for giving generously of his time to critique my slides.

Finally, my deepest gratitude goes to my mother, Gussie Garland, and my aunt, Nell Klinkman, for their support and encouragement.

Preface

I felt like a peeping Tom. I was watching a female cardinal busy at her toilette. I peered across a narrow inlet of water at the bottom of a wooded culvert and caught a glimpse of her reddish tail just as she flew from the water's edge. The thick tangle of tree roots protruding from the opposite bank almost hid her olive-gray sides from view.

As she snuggled in among the brambles to preen, I crouched behind a thorny bush to take full advantage of the show. Warily she looked in all directions to make sure no one was about, and then she proceeded to spread her red-tinged wings, like a geisha coyly unfolding her fan. Slowly, deliberately, she nibbled along the edge of each feather, until, grooming chores finished, she made her exit.

Still peeping through my thorny window, I was diverted by a flying burst of scarlet. The male cardinal, brilliant red plumage all awry, had just taken his turn at the bath. Too busy to groom every feather as the female had done, he simply shook himself fiercely all over, much the same as a dog often does to rearrange his fur. Then, with a *"chink,"* he flitted out of sight in the same direction as his mate.

Suddenly I realized that nature has not one window but many, and they are all around us.

Another day found me peering through a different sort of window—a beveled glass panel in a door leading from a spacious bedroom onto a redwood deck overlooking Lake Waco in Central Texas. This time I was seated in air-conditioned comfort inside a friend's home. Only inches outside this window was a seven-foot ficus in a large wooden planter. Nestled in its small branches was a loosely built nest. The face and body of a female cardinal were barely visible among the branches. She sat on the nest, quietly for the most part, her dark shoe-button eyes ever alert. Intermittently, she emitted a soft *"chink"* from her throat. After a few moments she moved to the side of the nest, and a wobbly, fuzzy head with bulging eyes appeared beneath her—a tiny baby cardinal only three days out of the egg, my friend told me.

With a louder "*chink,*" the tawny female flew from the nest, and almost instantly a male cardinal appeared from somewhere in the surrounding woods to take his turn there. In his beak was a large green caterpillar, which he stuffed into the gaping mouth of the baby bird. I couldn't believe such a tiny bird could consume such a large caterpillar.

Still peering through the glass door, I wondered what would happen next. The patient father sat on the side of the nest while the hungry nestling gulped its meal. After a short while, the parent lowered his head into the nest and gathered in his bill a small white fecal sac deposited there by the nestling, and he carried it into the woods. Soon the mother returned to resume her vigil at the nest.

Another "window" gave me a dappled view as I gazed through the tiny openings in a camouflage net that covered a makeshift blind. Barbara Garland and I were watching four young cardinals as they devoured sunflower seeds on a friend's patio. The young birds, with varying shades of brown and red decorating their bodies, seemed to be of slightly different ages. One was almost golden brown and had no hint of red. I assumed this was a female. Another had tinges of red in its tail and wings, and I decided it was an older male cousin. The other two were plain brown all over with dark bills. It was impossible to determine their sex. They pecked at seeds that had spilled from the hanging feeder where House Finches were feeding above them.

One evening at dusk my spotting scope opened yet another window. As I scanned a lake shoreline, a crimson flash caught my eye. A male cardinal had just landed at water's edge. Slowly he dipped his beak to fill it with the refreshing liquid. He thrust his head back sharply so the water could trickle down his throat. In an instant he was gone. His tiny footprints were the only evidence he left behind. I was struck anew by his beauty and remarkable charm. Is it any wonder that the Northern Cardinal is one of America's favorite birds?

Through the pages of this book I hope to create many windows through which you may view the cardinal. First you will discover how the bird got its name and in what types of habitat and in what parts of the country it may be found. Through another of nature's "windows," you may view the seasons in the

life of this beautiful red bird. Beginning with January you will have your first close-up look when the male stakes out the territory in which he and his mate will breed and raise their young in the spring. You will watch as the pair go through their mating rituals, as they select their nesting site, and as the female constructs the nest. The birds, though sometimes facing adversity, will still be there, after having a second brood (and perhaps even a third and fourth), in midsummer.

You will learn about their favorite foods so that you can attract cardinals to your feeding stations. You will discover that during the fall molt, cardinals become secretive and almost totally silent while they exchange old feathers for new. Then suddenly their stark beauty reappears against a winter landscape when the tribe gathers, and flocks remain together until late December. When January rolls around once more, pairs of birds separate themselves from the flock, and a male cardinal surprises you with his long-awaited wake-up call on a cold winter morning. Then America's favorite "redbird" and his mate once again return to their chosen nesting ground—their land of beginning again—perchance, if you're lucky, in your own backyard.

Through another window you will see how the popularity of this flamboyant red bird affects American culture—as state symbol, athletic mascot, and object of art and literature. Finally, you will see why Big Red has become known as "the bird of Christmas."

The Cardinal

The Northern Cardinal is America's favorite "redbird."

The cardinal is one of the jewels of our bird-fauna, being incomparable in the combination of proud bearing and gaudy coloring, and unexcelled in certain qualities of its song. Few birds impart their haunts with such life, beauty, and poetry as this brilliant songster, one of the most famous among birds and highly prized by all bird lovers.

—Henry Nehrling (1896)

Introduction

People have been attracted to the beauty of the cardinal for centuries. Even in states and countries where the bird does not occur, it is known and admired. Among the first published pictures of a cardinal was a work in 1599 by Aldrovandi, the director of a botanical garden in Bologna, Italy. Since the bird was drawn from life, it apparently was captured in the New World and taken alive to the artist in Italy. Another early well-known drawing of the "Virginian Nightingale" appeared almost a century later in Francis Willughby's *Ornithologiae libri tres* (London, 1676). The bird's popularity, then, seems to be long-standing.

Cardinalis cardinalis is classified in the family Emberizidae. Some of America's finest songsters are in this family, including the Northern Cardinal.

The cardinal got its name from the Latin word *cardo,* "the hinge of a door." Figuratively this meant "important," or something upon which an object or an idea hinged or depended. The cardinal of the Roman Catholic Church is an important figure upon whose decisions matters of administration and policy depend, and he wears a red hat and robe. Hence Carollus Linnaeus, the famous eighteenth-century Swedish botanist known as the Father of Taxonomy, chose to ascribe the name *cardinal* to the bird whose plumage matches the radiant color of the papal robes of the church's cardinal. Through the centuries the name has stuck.

Throughout its range the Northern Cardinal has many colloquial nicknames. In the state of Virginia it is designated the "Virginia cardinal," "Virginia nightingale," and "Virginia redbird." Some Virginians have even gone so far as to call it an FFV—a member of one of the First Families of Virginia.

In the bluegrass state it is called the "Kentucky cardinal." John James Audubon, one of America's most renowned naturalists, once lived in Henderson, Kentucky, where Audubon State Park was named in his honor. Here two bronze plaques

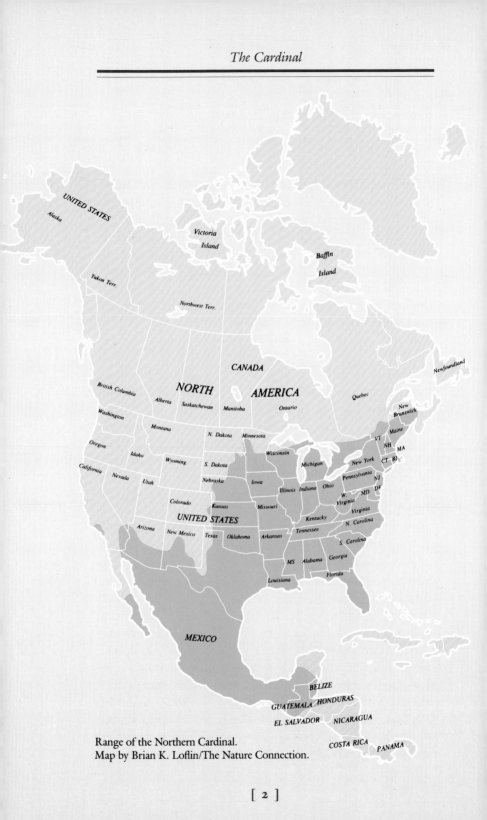

Range of the Northern Cardinal.
Map by Brian K. Loflin/The Nature Connection.

commemorate the early explorer, ornithologist, and artist. Each of the plaques is decorated with images of cardinals, one of Audubon's favorite songbirds. In describing the cardinal in his journals, he said, "In richness of plumage, elegance of motion, and strength of song, this species surpasses all its kindred in the United States."

In other localities the bird is known as "cardinal grosbeak," "cardinal bird," "Big Red," "topknot redbird," and "crested redbird." However, the most popular moniker by which this scarlet beauty is affectionately known is simply "redbird."

The cardinal is a year-round nonmigratory resident from the Dakotas, southern Ontario, and Nova Scotia south to the Gulf Coast, and from southern Texas westward through Arizona and southward through Mexico as far as Guatemala and Honduras. The Northern Cardinal was introduced in Hawaii in 1929 and now is well established there. It also occurs in southwestern California and in Bermuda as an introduced species.

In the *Field Guide to Mexican Birds,* Roger Tory Peterson and Edward Chalif mention the Pacific Coast form *Cardinalis carnea* that ranges from Colima to Oaxaca. Formerly it was considered a distinct species known as the Long-crested Cardinal. Most authorities, however, now agree it is not.

South America claims seven species of birds with *cardinal* in their names. Only one of them, the Vermilion Cardinal (*Cardinalis phoeniceus*), is in the same genus as our familiar Northern Cardinal. It has a limited range in the northern extremes of Venezuela and Colombia. The male is all red with a long upright crest. The female has brown upparts and a small red crest. Her underparts are ochraceous buff. The other six South American "cardinals" are the Yellow Cardinal (*Gubernatrix cristata*), whose range includes most of Argentina and Uruguay; the Red-crested Cardinal (*Paroaria coronata*), which lives throughout Bolivia, Paraguay, Uruguay, and most of Argentina; the Red-cowled Cardinal (*Paroaria dominicana*), found within the northeastern portions of Brazil; the Red-capped Cardinal (*Paroaria gularis*) of northwestern South America; the Crimson-fronted Cardinal (*Paroaria baeri*) of interior Brazil; and, finally, the Yellow-billed Cardinal (*Paroaria capitata*).

Their range extends from just north of Paraguay southward through the northern half of Argentina.

Granted, all these exotic South American "cardinals" are colorful, but none compares with America's favorite flamboyant redbird. Paul R. Ehrlich said it well: "Birds are, hands down, the most colorful terrestrial vertebrates—only insects and coral reef fishes rival them among animals." The cardinal has to be close to the top of the list of most colorful birds. Indeed, many people have become much interested in *all* birds by first being attracted by the beauty of the cardinal.

It doesn't take a bird expert to identify a male Northern Cardinal. Whether a person knows much about birds or not, almost everyone who lives within its range recognizes the male cardinal's brilliant red plumage, its crest, and its clearly whistled songs. From his perky topknot, which he raises and lowers at will, to the tip of his long slender tail, the male cardinal is covered with crimson feathers. The feathers on his back and scapulars are edged with brown or gray, giving his back a somewhat duller appearance than the rest of him. His iris is dark reddish brown, brown, or hazel. A roguish black mask surrounds his strong, cone-shaped coral-red bill. Even his feet and legs are dark red.

By contrast, his female counterpart is soft grayish brown on the back. She shows variable tinges of red on her crest, tail, and short rounded wings. There is an area of darker feathers around her bill, but nothing like the male's distinctive black mask. Her underparts are warm pinkish brown, and her bill is about the same color as the male's.

Since the male weighs slightly more than the female, he may appear to be a little larger than she is in any given pair. The average weight of the male is 45.4 grams; that of the female, 43.9 grams.

The unattractive juvenile looks as if someone made a mistake when applying its color. The only thing about it that is cardinal-like is its shape. Its identity is sometimes a mystery to those not familiar with the somewhat plain markings. It is browner overall than the female and has a blackish bill. Its crest is not quite as long as that of its parents. The plumage of the immature male is tinged with red. When fall arrives, the young cardinals of both sexes begin to molt, and one month later, after acquiring their first winter's plumage, they look exactly like their parents.

Cherokee legend has it that the cardinal was originally an all-brown bird, much like the juvenile just described. In the story, the little brown bird was most unhappy with his dingy feathers. All the other birds of the forest were brightly colored, and they made fun of the ugly one. One day in his wanderings he came upon a wolf that had been tricked by a raccoon. While the wolf was sleeping, the raccoon placed mud packs on his eyes so that when he awoke he couldn't open them. When the brown bird saw the plight of the wolf, he befriended him by pecking the mud away from his eyes. The wolf was so grateful that he rewarded the unattractive bird for his kindness by telling him where there was a rock with streaks of bright red paint running through it. According to the legend, the bird found the rock and painted himself. Ever since, he has been red and considered the most beautiful bird in the forest.

There are two other all-red birds of the North American forest that might be mistaken for the cardinal: the Summer Tanager (*Piranga rubra*) and the Hepatic Tanager (*Piranga flava*). Both are slightly smaller than the cardinal. The Summer Tanager averages 7¾ inches in length and the Hepatic Tanager 8 inches, but the cardinal—typically 8¾ inches—is longer. Although the observer may think at first that these birds are cardinals, he soon sees that the tanagers have no crest and no black mask; too, they are migratory. The Summer Tanager lives in the southern United States and the Hepatic Tanager in the Southwest only during breeding season. The Northern Cardinal is present in those regions year-round.

Next of kin to the cardinal is the Pyrrhuloxia (*Cardinalis sinuatus*), a resident of the Southwest. It is sometimes called the "Texas cardinal." Its song is similar to that of the Northern Cardinal, and its body has the general shape and size of the cardinal. When seen in silhouette the two may seem identical.

Cherokee legend has it that the cardinal was originally an all-brown bird, much like this juvenile.

In some localities the cardinal is known as "topknot redbird" and "crested redbird."

Close inspection reveals that the male Pyrrhuloxia is an exquisite shade of gray overall, with red on his face where the cardinal is black. He has red in the tip of the crest and on the wings and a generous spilling of rose color on the belly and tail. His bill is orange-yellow in contrast to the cardinal's coral-red. The female Pyrrhuloxia is mostly gray and shows very little, if any, red anywhere.

Where the territories of *Cardinalis cardinalis* and *Cardinalis sinuatus* overlap—in southwestern Texas, southern New Mexico, southeastern Arizona, and in Mexico—a bird-watcher may have difficulty in determining which is which, because their songs as well as their silhouettes are similar. One must carefully examine the face and bill of the cardinal look-alike, Pyrrhuloxia. A surprising difference exists in the shapes of their bills. The Pyrrhuloxia looks as if it has been in a fight with a heavyweight boxing champion—and lost. Its parrotlike bill is thick and strongly curved, giving it the appearance of having been almost flattened.

The Northern Cardinal is found in a variety of settings, from the Everglades of South Florida to the evergreens of the North to the arid desert lands of the Southwest and Mexico. The cardinal has adapted to habitats over wide areas in both temperate and subtropical climates. The species seems as much at home in a woodland edge or desert shrub, in a streamside thicket or dingy chaparral, as in an elaborately landscaped New England urban garden or the preserves of the Deep South.

Have you ever wondered where cardinals go each day after they feed voraciously in your backyard? From early morning until late evening they are frequent diners at feeding stations. They linger awhile on the ground or on low feeding trays, fill themselves with sunflower seeds you have placed there for them, and then disappear. Where do they go? If you followed the low, pumping flight of one, you would find yourself in a surprising assortment of places.

If you live in the South your cardinal might lead you into a pine forest with deciduous undergrowth. In Florida's Everglades I followed a cardinal onto Snake Bight Trail, which led me deep into a mangrove swamp. There thick swarms of mosquitoes soon forced me to give up pursuit of the bird. In the Southwest and in Mexico you might follow your winged guide into desert shrub or chaparral as I once did. Near San Fernando in Tamaulipas, I saw a male cardinal with an insect in its mouth. I assumed it was about to feed its young. Curiosity led me to try to locate the nest to photograph it, but it was not to be. Instead of locating the nest, I soon found myself knee-deep in thorny vegetation. I could go no farther.

In other places you may find yourself in a brushy border, in thick tangles of greenbrier, in a streamside thicket, or possibly even on a country roadside. Roadsides can be quite dangerous for the bird if it lands too close to the roadway. Thousands of birds are inadvertently killed each year by passing cars. Once photographer Barbara Garland found a dead female cardinal beside a country road. She stopped to watch when she noticed the bird's mate flying back and forth above the lifeless form.

So you see, if you *could* follow your favorite redbird when it leaves your garden, you would find it at home in a number of interesting and varied habitats. Soon you would realize there *is* life—and death—for the cardinal outside your backyard.

To everything there is a season, and a time to every purpose under the heaven.

—Ecclesiastes 3 : 1

PART I

Seasons in the Life of the Cardinal

The male bursts into flight in a blur of crimson.

A bird's song is an audible fence. It announces to rivals that the singer's territory is taken and will be defended.

—Paul A. Johnsgard

January: Establishing Territory

*O*n a bleak morning in January, one may awaken to the sound of a male cardinal in full song. Indeed, this is the season in the life of the cardinal that may best be characterized by song. This is the time during which the bird constructs an audible barrier that designates a few acres as his territory. Just as the bricklayer constructs a wall, laying brick on brick, the male cardinal delimits the invisible boundaries of his territory, laying note on note.

Territory is defined as any area defended by a bird against other birds of its own kind. It may be roughly classified into two categories: breeding territory and nonbreeding territory. The commonest type is breeding territory—that used for mating, nesting, and feeding of the adults and the young. Once a pair of birds claims a territory, they usually remain there at least until their offspring are independent. Nonbreeding territory may be used for foraging away from the breeding grounds or for nighttime roosting—a place to sleep during the winter months, for example. This type is usually defended just as fiercely as the breeding territory.

Territory size varies widely among bird species, from mere inches to several miles. Extremes may be illustrated by the average thirty-six square miles defended by the Golden Eagle and the one square foot defended by the Common Murre. The eagle's territory is multipurpose and is spread out because its chief food—small mammals—is thinly dispersed over a large area. The murre is a seabird that nests in large colonies on rocky ledges overlooking the sea. Its territory is so small that sometimes birds touch one another while sitting on their nests. Northern Cardinals, in comparison, defend an area from less than two to ten acres in size. In this plot of ground there may be other species of birds—mockingbirds, wrens, or jays, for example—but there will be only one pair of cardinals.

Cardinals, and other birds, use song to proclaim their territory. In a study of cardinals conducted in the Woodway

While in full song, the cardinal raises its crest, giving the bird character and revealing its full beauty.

Ravine, Waco, Texas, from 1965 to 1990, biology professor Frederick R. Gehlbach discovered that territorial singing begins between January 8 and 22. Arthur Cleveland Bent describes the cardinal as a persistent singer throughout most of the year. Amelia R. Laskey says that full song by the males usually extends from February to September, and by the females, from March until July or August.

No matter what the date, it is pleasant indeed to awake on an early January morning when a Northern Cardinal's jubilant song invites you to see the sunrise. The sound is especially welcome when you remember that it has been a long, long time since the sweet voice was heard. The birds have been almost totally silent since they went into their postbreeding molt—the time when they lose all their worn-out feathers and replace them with a fine new set after nesting duties are completed.

While in full song, the cardinal raises its crest, giving the bird character and revealing its full beauty. On a January morning the casual listener may not realize that the bold and beautiful crimson male, dressed in his splendid new winter coat, is actually constructing an audible fence with his singing just as surely as if he were building a wall. Though his barrier is invisible to the human eye, it is quite real to other male cardinals competing for territory. To them the singer is announcing that these few acres are preempted by him, and interlopers should not cross over into his space.

Song is only one element in avian communication. Basically birds have two modes: (*a*) visual displays, or body language, which I will discuss later, and (*b*) vocal displays, generally classified in two categories—songs and call notes.

Song mainly consists of syllables or sounds consistently repeated in a specific pattern. These songs are usually sung, with some exceptions, only by territorial males during breeding season. The Northern Cardinal female is one of those exceptions. She is as accomplished a singer as her male counterpart. Her song is softer than his, is sung somewhat less frequently, and is often used to defend their territory against invasions by other female cardinals. Her songs and call notes also bond her to her mate.

When do cardinals sing? One may be heard singing with as much vigor on a subfreezing day during a Minnesota winter as on a blazing hot day in the Southwest's summer heat. Some birds, such as the Carolina Wren, sing year-round, but this is not the norm. Most birds in the Temperate Zone virtually end their singing after the nesting season, especially during their postbreeding molt. Frequently during this off period, however, some birds, including the cardinal, sing what is called a soft "whisper" or muted song. With audibility limited to no more than about twenty yards, sometimes this whisper song is too soft to be heard, which leads bird-watchers to think the birds are not singing at all.

Some birds sing all day long and into the night. The Northern Mockingbird is notorious for being a tireless nocturnal virtuoso. It may surprise some cardinal devotees to discover that cardinals, too, occasionally sing at night. I have been awakened at 1:00 A.M. on many a spring night when the cardinals of our neighborhood joined the chorus of the mockingbird's nightly recital.

Henry Nehrling, a writer of the nineteenth century, said that when cardinals hear mockingbirds from far and near rivaling in their singing, "the Cardinals cannot withstand the temptation of joining the chorus of this nocturnal concert. At first one utters a few notes, which slowly increase in power, becoming louder, fuller, and more varied. . . . I have heard this incomparably enchanting concert of Nature not only when the moon poured her light on the landscape, but also during very dark nights." Nehrling's favorite place in which to observe cardinals was along the Texas coast in April. He said, "The spring and summer nights in the Gulf region are indescribably charming and bewitchingly beautiful when Mockingbirds and Cardinals join in their fascinating night concerts."

John Burroughs noted in one of his journals, "Along the Potomac I have heard the Virginia cardinal whistle so loudly and persistently in the treetops above, that sleeping after four o'clock (A.M.) was out of the question."

No matter when they sound off, the quality of vocalizations in different species of birds ranges from the sublime to the ridiculous. What could be more sublime than the ethereal flutelike notes of a Wood Thrush floating through the eerie half-light of dawn or dusk in an eastern forest? Or what could be more ridiculous than the "*Gallump! Gallump! Gallump!*" of an American Bittern hiding within the reeds of a marsh? To me the sweet-voiced song of the Northern Cardinal falls very near the sublime end of the spectrum of avian vocalizations. Some observers think the notes of the cardinal are almost equal to those of the Nightingale, the bird considered the "sweetest feathered minstrel of Europe."

The cardinal has many different songs. Indeed, at one time it was a much sought-after caged bird—even more so than canaries—because its plumage and musical ability are equally brilliant. In the nineteenth century, cardinals were trapped by the thousands in the South during winter and taken to markets in the North. In addition, thousands were shipped annually to Europe where they were regarded as caged birds of the highest rank. Nehrling wrote about this in 1896: "This glory of our bird-fauna deserves everywhere careful protection and fostering. Stringent laws should be passed by the legislatures of the Southern States for the protection of birds, and these laws should be strictly enforced." Thankfully, since the Migratory Bird Treaty Act was enacted in 1918, our native birds are protected by federal laws. Now the birds and their songs can be enjoyed only as they were meant to be—in the wild—and unconfined.

Widely distributed species, such as the cardinal, often have pronounced local variations or accents in their song much like the distinctive dialects spoken by people in different parts of the country. Although the cardinal has two dozen or more variations in its song, each one has a typically cardinal quality no matter which dialect the bird is using. Something about the voice quality and the general phraseology leaves no doubt in the mind, no matter where listeners are when they hear it, that this is a cardinal singing. Some visitors to Hawaii are surprised and delighted upon their first arrival in the islands when they hear a Northern Cardinal's rich familiar song. Of course, there, it may be interpreted by the natives as sounding more like "*Le'a-le'a!*" (the Hawaiian word for "cheer" or "joy") than "*What cheer-cheer-cheer!*"

Call notes are normally short sounds that lack a specific pattern. They include all vocalizations made by birds that cannot be described as song. The most familiar call note made by cardinals is the short, metallic "*chink*" or "*chip*" often heard around backyard feeders. This note may be uttered in many different situations to convey different messages, such as an aggressive warning to an intruding male. Or the bird may simply be trying to stay in touch with its mate, to say it is going to roost, for instance. Or the call note may be given as an alarm to warn the other of some lurking danger such as the presence of a predator.

During fall and winter I often hear that warning call near my backyard feeders when a Sharp-shinned Hawk suddenly appears there to look for an easy meal of some small unsuspecting bird. Simply by the cardinal's tone of voice, I know it signals the presence of the hawk, and certainly the other birds know, because they immediately scatter for cover. (Gehlbach reports that a male cardinal recently released from banding was caught by a Sharp-shin, but the feisty cardinal fought off the hawk in five seconds flat. Could it be that the cardinal was prepared for a fight because of the warning calls of some other bird?) In short, the call note serves a dual purpose: to convey a variety of messages between mates and to warn other birds about intruders.

We humans tend to listen to bird songs with our aesthetic sense, and whether we understand their meaning or not, we enjoy what we hear. Although countless studies have examined what motivates a bird to sing, they all seem to indicate that males' songs have two primary functions: (*a*) to attract a female of the same species and (*b*) to drive away other males of the same species. It's as simple as that. In other words, the male singer is saying, "I am an available male who would like to have a mate" and "I own this territory from which I sing, and I dare any male of like species to invade these boundaries!" The female bird that sings is saying, in essence, "I like what I hear, I accept your invitation, and all other females of my kind may as well stay away."

Each and every species has its own unique song that is different from the songs of every other species. Even individual birds within a species have their own unique songs. Some authors claim that each song is as distinctive as a fingerprint. With practice and experience, a person can learn to recognize birds by their songs. Knowledgeable birders don't even have to *see* the birds to know what species are present. The songs give them a prescriptive clue to the birds' identities.

Novices, on the other hand, may encounter utter confusion, when on a spring morning they stroll through the park and try to differentiate between the diverse warbler songs that surround them. They should not despair. Records, tapes, and compact discs can aid anyone learning to recognize bird songs. The Laboratory of Ornithology at Cornell University in Ithaca, New York, and ABA Sales in Colorado Springs, Colorado, offer such recordings.

Even though the casual human observer may not be able to tell the difference between the songs of a Carolina Wren and a Northern Cardinal, the birds know the difference. Some researchers believe that a bird responds only to the song of its own species. According to them, a cardinal will not respond even to a well-executed imitation of its song when given by a mockingbird. Other ornithologists claim that a cardinal will respond to a whistled imitation of its territorial call. At any rate, since most bird songs are species-specific, the difference in the songs ensures that females will mate only with members of their own species and thus prevent hybridization.

Have you noticed that different species of birds prefer different heights from which to sing? Some songbirds occasionally sing from the ground. The American Robin is one of these. But most birds prefer a perch that is high above the ground. Cardinals prefer the lofty places like treetops and high utility wires. According to the section of the country in which you observe them, they may be seen singing from atop a tall pine tree in the Southeast or from a giant saguaro in the Sonoran Desert.

The cardinals in our neighborhood in Central Texas, for example, prefer the TV antenna on the rooftop of our next-door neighbor's house. From there, on most mornings from midwinter through the summer, our resident male redbird delivers a wake-up call to the entire neighborhood: *"What cheer-cheer-cheer!"* he calls. And from somewhere in the backyard his mate answers, matching his song, phrase for phrase, *"What cheer-cheer-cheer!"* This duetting is called "countersinging" and occurs mainly in permanently paired species in which both sexes stay together year-round. It strengthens the bond between them and lets others of their kind know that this territory is occupied and will be defended at all costs.

Sometimes a male from an adjoining territory countersings, following and matching the phrases of the first male. This type of countersinging between males is often interspersed with flights into one another's space. When this happens, the intruding male is chased away by the resident male.

Occasionally, an unmated female attempts to invade another's territory. When this occurs, the resident female chases her away while her mate observes the action passively. Cardinals usually are tolerant of the opposite sex and do not become involved in joint efforts with their mates to drive off intruders.

It takes a good imagination to put words to the musical notes of birds. Numerous writers have described the songs of cardinals in various ways. *"What cheer-cheer-cheer!"* is a popular interpretation of one of the most familiar of cardinal songs.

Overall, a cardinal's song is a variable series of loud, rich, whistled notes sometimes sounding like, *"Wheer, wheer, wheer. Whoit, whoit, whoit, whoit."* The first three notes descend in pitch, and the *"whoit"* notes rise sharply and are delivered more rapidly.

Another series of phrases may be interpreted as *"Hew whoit whoit whoit,"* or *"Whit-chew, whit-chew, whit whit whit"* or *"Cue, cue, cue."*

At other times we hear *"Birdy, birdy, birdy!"* or *"Purty, purty, purty!"* as if the bird is admitting to the world he knows how beautiful he is. No matter what interpretation one ascribes to the songs of the cardinal, hearing *"What cheer-cheer-cheer!"* does help brighten an otherwise bleak day in the dead of winter.

The fact remains that whether perched on utility wires strung alongside busy highways or in the lacy branches of cypress trees that line a pristine river, the brilliant red of a male Northern Cardinal and the cheery notes of its song capture our attention.

Have you ever wondered how long it takes a bird to sing its song? In 1958, Charles A. Hartshorne discovered that the primary song of most of the songbirds takes less than four seconds to execute. *Primary song* is defined as the vocalization most commonly heard in spring and summer when the bird is on its nesting territory. The longest fixed primary bird song he found was that of the Winter Wren, which lasted from eight to ten seconds. Hartshorne also found that the songs of the cardinal fall in the midlength category, varying from 1.8 to 4.2 seconds. Of course, these brief renditions are repeated at several-second intervals, giving the listener the impression of a much lengthier song.

In most species of birds, only the male sings, and only during the brief breeding season of spring and summer. But among cardinals, male and female sing equally well. And, although most authors report that the cardinal sings year-round, I have observed that the ones around our home are almost totally silent from the time they begin their fall molt until late December or early January. If they sing at all during this period, it is the soft whisper song described earlier. Consequently, one-third of the year we are deprived of their beautiful full song. That is one reason why the sound of a cardinal's clear tones is so welcome against the backdrop of a cold, drab morning in January—the time of beginning again for America's favorite redbird—when he builds his invisible boundary wall, laying note on note.

Birds increase their visits to feeders in harsh weather, particularly after snowfalls and ice storms that make natural foods inaccessible.

—Paul Ehrlich

Each species has its own method of courtship and breeding, a ritualized strategy for survival so deeply imbued in the genes that no individual bird has to figure out how it ought to proceed.

—Paul A. Johnsgard

February and March:
Winter Feeding, Range Expansion, and Courtship

The February sky was dark gray and looked ominous as sundown approached. By bedtime a cold rain began to fall. A heavy covering of snow, unusual for Central Texas, surprised my family and me the next morning. Suddenly, it seemed that the bird feeders in our backyard became *the place to visit* by all the birds for miles around. Birds that my family and I normally do not see on a daily basis joined the cardinals, Blue Jays, and Carolina Chickadees.

That day we observed a Brown Thrasher who came at least three times to bathe in the slush in the birdbath that had the consistency of an icy drink from the neighborhood convenience store. Dark-eyed Juncos by the dozens were at the back of the garden. A Harris' Sparrow and a White-crowned Sparrow, usually birds of the open country, on that day found sustenance in suburbia. A Rufous-sided Towhee scratched like a chicken in the tray of scratch feed.

I spent the entire day filling and refilling feeders and defrosting the birdbath every hour or so. The rest of the family, when they weren't helping me or playing in the snow, spent their time looking out the window at the ever-changing bird scene. The crimson robes of the male cardinals were by far the most stunning of this colorful array against the white background.

Winter Feeding and Range Expansion

Scenes such as the one just described are not unusual in backyards all across the land during the colder months of the year, and so we dub this the season for backyard bird-watchers to pour on the food for our bird friends.

There is no doubt that winter feeding stations are beneficial to birds, especially in the northern regions of the United States where weather can be extreme. They supply a food source when natural food is covered by ice or snow. However, a person doesn't really need a motive for feeding birds other than wanting to see them up close. And what better way to do this than to offer them food right outside the windows? At any rate, feeding birds is an interesting pastime that benefits not only the avian species, but also *Homo sapiens,* who so enjoys a close look at feathered wildlings.

At the age of seventy-four, my mother started feeding birds in her backyard. At that time she was so crippled with arthritis that she could not go out on field trips to see the birds she loved to watch. My family and I gave her a bird feeder and kept her supplied with seeds so the birds would come to her. The last four years of her life she spent many a pleasant hour sitting in her breakfast room and watching the birds outside the window. My youngest son was four years old when he first took an interest in watching the activity at our "bird window."

Why does feeding backyard birds have such a wide appeal to people of all ages? The answer may be that it brings life to the scene outside and adds color to our lives. Marjorie Valentine Adams, in *A Gift of Birds,* explains the appeal this way: "Birds do many of the things humans do, as we may see ourselves mirrored in some of their habits and actions. They can be comical, joyous, tender, fierce or puzzling, matching almost any basic human behavior."

I suppose people have been giving birds handouts as long as people have been watching birds. The practice came into vogue in the late 1800s, when numerous books were published on the subject of feeding birds. In his 1896 publication, Henry Nehrling said that cardinals came in numbers of five to ten to a feeding place he had arranged for various birds in the woods bordering his house in Missouri.

Feeding birds in North America began to increase dramatically in the early 1950s. Since then the practice has grown so rapidly that an estimated 82.5 million Americans now spend more than one-half billion dollars annually just to feed the birds. That means nearly half of the population over sixteen years of age feeds birds as a hobby. The data collected by the

U.S. Fish and Wildlife Service indicate that over 20 million new people began feeding wild birds between 1980 and 1985. Attracting birds to our yards with feeding stations is now second only to gardening in popularity as an outdoor pastime.

New Englanders are our most dedicated providers, with no less than 40 percent of the households of Amherst, Massachusetts, offering winter food for birds. One study showed that, overall, one in three North American households makes available an average of sixty pounds of supplemental seed each year. That's a lot of bird seed! For your money, one of the best-nourishing seeds to buy for your backyard birds is the small black oil sunflower seed. It provides more nutrition than the larger striped seeds. Cardinals love them, and so do numerous other species.

Some authorities believe this increased interest in winter feeding has expanded the range of certain species of birds. For example, in Audubon's day (1785–1851) the cardinal was considered a southern bird and was rarely seen as far north as Philadelphia. By 1895 its range reached the Great Lakes, and by 1910 the cardinal was in southern Ontario and along the southern portion of the Hudson River. In more recent years, cardinals have become common backyard breeding birds as far north as some parts of southern Canada. During the 1989 Christmas Bird Count, an annual census that attempts to determine the early winter distribution of our native birds, counters in Ontario tallied 6,303 Northern Cardinals in some sixty areas. That same year, 3 cardinals were counted in Manitoba, 4 in Nova Scotia, 7 in New Brunswick, and 125 in the province of Quebec. (These figures in no way reflect the total number of cardinals in these areas. They merely indicate the number counted on a particular day in those particular areas.)

Other authorities explain the cardinal's range expansion by temperature and moisture conditions in certain parts of the country. For example, Terry Root, in her analysis of Christmas Bird Count data spanning the winters from 1962/1963 through 1971/1972, discovered that, to the north, the cardinal in winter is found where the average minimum January temperature is above five degrees Fahrenheit. And, according to her findings, the western edge of the main wintering area of cardinals is influenced by moisture, with the species frequenting only those regions that receive more than sixteen inches of annual precipitation.

One of the most intriguing theories offered for the cardinal's push northward is one espoused by Roger Tory Peterson, author, bird artist, and guru of North American bird-watchers. Formerly the cardinal's range was bounded on the east by the Hudson River. With that in mind, consider Peterson's idea that it was the building of the George Washington Bridge in 1931 that enabled the cardinals to cross the Hudson. He explains that since they are not highly migratory birds, it is reasonable to assume that after the bridge was built cardinals were able to cross the river without having to make long sustained flights. Now they can make their way slowly across the river by resting from time to time on the struts of the bridge.

John V. Dennis, well-known authority on feeding birds, agrees with those who say the cardinal's northward expansion has largely been made possible by the availability of food at feeding stations. He says, "Ability to adapt to a variety of habitats, and especially to advantages offered by humans, is a prime factor in the cardinal's success." The truth is, no one really knows for sure why cardinals now occur where once they did not. Whatever the reasons, that brilliant flash of red is now one of the most common and most welcome sights around feeders throughout the bird's range.

Indeed, the Northern Cardinal, more than any other bird, has come to symbolize bird feeding. A buyer for a major bookstore chain once told a publisher that he would not buy a particular bird book for sale in his stores because it did not have a cardinal on the cover. How many books have you seen on the subject of attracting birds that have a picture of a male cardinal on the front? I counted six in my own personal library. The books without them would be easier to count. Or how many bags of birdseed do you see on your grocer's shelves without an artist's rendition of a cardinal decorating the package?

Granted, the bright color of this bird attracts the reader's or shopper's attention, but the cardinal won its place in advertising in ways that have nothing to do with color. It is one of the first birds to appear at feeders in the morning, sometimes before daylight, and one of the last to leave in the evening, often after dark. Incidentally, Texas bird-watcher Fred Gehlbach suspects this may be the reason cardinals are highly susceptible to predation by Eastern Screech-Owls, who feed at those times of day. He reports that cardinals are the second most common resident species eaten by screech owls (behind the House Sparrow), and 71 percent of these are males, a statistically significant number indicating male boldness. He cites one example of a male cardinal that was banded on February 9, 1978, and found as stored food in a screech owl nest only a thousand feet away a little more than a year later on May 3, 1979.

The reward for maintaining feeding stations throughout the summer months as well as winter comes when cardinal parents bring their offspring there to teach them the advantages of a readily available food supply. It is feasible to assume that since some cardinals have as many as three, four, or five broods of young in one nesting season (depending on the area of the country), the enjoyment of watching them at close range may be sustained over an extended period of time throughout the summer months.

I keep feeders well stocked throughout the year, and by the first of August each year I have usually already seen the juveniles of at least three broods from the same pair of cardinals. It is interesting to watch them, because soon you can recognize the different individuals by the way they act or by a feather that is out of place or some other distinguishing feature. Once I observed a juvenile cardinal that fed on the ground every day until he discovered above him the hanging feeder that contained more seeds than he could find on the ground. As soon as he made the discovery he started going directly to the feeder without first checking out the ground-level seed supply. He dared any other species, such as the ubiquitous House Sparrow, even to alight on the feeder. It became his own personal property. Over a period of several days I observed that the only other bird he would tolerate on the feeder while he was there was an adult female. I assumed she was his own mother.

Cardinals' short, heavy beaks crack seeds with strong adductor muscles that enable them to handle larger and tougher seeds that birds with smaller bills cannot crack. The grooved upper mandible holds the seed while the sharp-edged lower mandible moves forward and crushes and husks the seed. The bird then swallows the inner nutmeat.

Popular belief has it that cardinals eat only sunflower seeds, but this is not true. They accept with equal fervor cracked corn; white millet; nutmeats of all kinds; the seeds of squash, watermelon, pumpkin, and cantaloupe; and other grains, such as wheat and barley.

Sylvia Montroy, a writer who lives in New Jersey, relates a charming story of her family's discovery of the cardinal's affinity for squash seeds. She recalls that one day while preparing acorn squash for dinner, she decided, on a whim, to place the seeds in a pan on the deck within six feet of a sliding glass door to their family room. For several months the seeds remained untouched. Finally, a male cardinal investigated the pan's contents and liked what he tasted. His mate soon joined him, and after that the Montroy family ate acorn squash far more often than they would have chosen, just so they could provide the birds with their preference in treats.

Montroy said she soon realized that in order to keep the cardinals continually supplied with the seeds her family would have to eat squash every day. Since they were not prepared to do that, she started ordering the seeds through a seed catalog. Though she paid a high price for them, she said it was worth every cent, because when breeding season rolled around her family was treated to an educational aspect of the project she had not counted on—the parents teaching their offspring independence. One day a fledgling could not figure out what to do with the large uncracked seed its parent placed in its mouth. After rotating it in its beak, scrubbing it against the deck floor, and dropping and retrieving it time after time without success, the young bird finally gave up and in desperation ate a geranium petal from a potted plant nearby instead. Squash, anyone?

Some cardinals have been observed feeding on nectar. Mary W. Wible of Ocala, Florida, reported to the *Auk* (April 1974) that she and a friend saw a pair of cardinals habitually feed on the blossoms of shrimp plants. Wible and her friend first noticed this practice when they saw a male cardinal eating blossoms that had fallen on the ground. The male then flew up into the dense foliage of the plants, where he was seen plucking the flowers and eating a portion of them before dropping what remained to the ground. Soon he was joined by a female cardinal, who followed his example. When they were finished, Wible examined the blossoms and determined that the birds had eaten only the small greenish white capsule at the base of the calyx, which was missing from the blossoms the birds had dropped on the ground. This capsule is sticky to the touch and sweet to the taste. So it would appear that hummingbirds are not the only avian species that visit plants for their nectar. At least in Florida, cardinals also enjoy this natural treat.

In a letter to Arthur Cleveland Bent, the Rev. J. J. Murray once noted a pair of cardinals that visited the holes made in a maple tree by sapsuckers. It was early in March, when the sap was running freely, and, according to Murray, the birds were drinking greedily.

In a paper on the food of grosbeaks, W. L. McAtee gives the results attained from the examination of nearly five hundred stomachs of Northern Cardinals. His examination showed that three-tenths of a cardinal's diet is animal and seven-tenths vegetable. Included in the animal part was a portion of a field mouse that one male cardinal had consumed.

Additionally, cardinals are easily attracted to mealworms, a welcome supplement, especially during nesting. The adult birds bring them to the nestlings. You may ask how a supply of mealworms can be obtained. You can raise them at home, or they may be purchased from bait or pet shops. If all else fails, ask the nearest biology teacher for a supply catalog from which they may be ordered.

Though cardinals are mainly seed eaters, they also eat a variety of insects that are considered harmful to crops. The pesky green caterpillars that defoliate oaks and descend to the ground on thin webs are sometimes caught by cardinals in typical flycatcher fashion. Other birds, like Yellow-rumped Warblers and

Cedar Waxwings, practice this type of food gathering, but they are notably winter visitors, rather than permanent residents like the cardinals.

Northern Cardinals eat more than fifty kinds of beetles, cicadas, dragonflies, leafhoppers, treehoppers, aphids, scale insects, ants, sawflies, termites, grasshoppers, crickets, caterpillars, codling moths, and cutworms. They also eat wood borers, fireflies, billbugs, and plant lice. This impressive array of insects on the cardinal's menu is enough to entitle the bird to the esteem of farmers and gardeners alike. Indeed, insects make up almost one-third of a cardinal's diet.

Like most insectivorous birds, cardinals love suet and suet mixes, too. Try this recipe that is a delight to cardinals as well as to many other kinds of birds that come to winter feeding stations, but remember it is recommended as a winter food only. In warm weather the oil from such a mixture can result in infection of feather follicles. A safe summer recipe appears on p. 55.

Recipe for Suet/Peanut Butter Mixture
(Winter Recipe)

1 cup of grease
1 cup of water
2 or 3 tablespoons of sugar (optional)
2 cups of cornmeal or oatmeal
½ cup crunchy peanut butter

The grease can be that which is melted out of suet scraps, or it can be waste fats from cooking, bacon grease, or lard. Heat the first four ingredients together until the mixture thickens. Remove from heat and add peanut butter. After cooling, place globs of this into holes drilled in a small log that can be hung in a tree. Make sure the log has a perch on it for the cardinals. A dowel pin can be used as a perch. Be prepared to fill the log often on cold days. Store the remaining mixture in the refrigerator.

Some authorities believe an increased interest in winter feeding has expanded the range of the Northern Cardinal.

Log feeder for suet and peanut butter mixture.
Drawing by Sam Osborne.

In addition to cardinals, a variety of other birds love this mixture, including chickadees, titmice, jays, woodpeckers, wrens, Ruby-crowned Kinglets, American Goldfinches, Purple Finches, Pine Siskins, and Yellow-rumped and Orange-crowned Warblers.

I first began feeding birds in my backyard in 1975. Since then, over forty species have come to the smorgasbord spread for them there. In addition, I have recorded well over one hundred species of birds sighted from our property, either feeding or flying overhead. Out of all those species, the cardinal remains our family favorite.

A few years after I started this feeding project my oldest son was visiting at home. He and I were sitting in the backyard watching a family of cardinals, and he commented, "Mom, your yard is virtually a bird sanctuary now, isn't it?" Up until then I had not thought of it as such; but, yes, it is. In order for this to happen in your yard, four basic ingredients are required: food, water, shelter, and a window. The first three ingredients are for the birds; the window is for you. A friend once told me, "What *I* can see is what *they* get." He saw no purpose in placing a bird feeder out of his line of vision. Neither do I.

Birds need water for drinking as well as for bathing to keep their plumage in tip-top condition both in summer and winter. Anything from an upside-down garbage can lid to an elaborate birdbath with a flowing fountain will do. Like small children, some birds, including cardinals, enjoy bathing in lawn sprinklers, and like watching children, watching cardinals can be quite entertaining.

Birds need shelter (or cover) for protection from weather and from predators and for a place to rest and raise their young. Existing plants, trees, shrubs, or homemade brush piles serve this purpose.

You need the window through which to view the scene now animated with birds going about the business of their daily lives. Through this window you may be privy to the most intimate of cardinal behavior that begins to unfold during this season of the year. Once the stage is set, up with the curtain and on with the show.

Shortly after Barbara Garland started feeding birds in her yard, she witnessed a small drama when she began to watch the behavior of a pair of cardinals. She first noticed the male because when he flew to a tree to perch he seemed unsteady and flopped around before gaining equilibrium. At first she thought he had an injured wing, but after the bird landed he seemed normal except that he sat very low on the limb and pumped his tail in un-cardinal-like fashion.

Finally, after several months of observing this behavior, Barbara discovered the reason for his unbalanced landing act. One day when he landed on the birdbath with his back to her, he leaned forward to get a drink. When he did, his right leg extended backward, and it was clearly apparent that the bird was missing his right foot.

Granted, this is not so unusual. A lot of birds meet with misfortune. The bizarre aspect of this story is that the male's mate was also minus her right foot. Of course, there is no way to know how or why both birds of this mated pair had the same handicap. Was it genetic? Was it accidental? No one knows. One can only speculate. Barbara observed the same two birds

Through your window you may view birds going about the business of their daily lives.

around her feeders for two years in a row, and they raised normal offspring through two breeding seasons. Had she not been feeding birds in her yard, she would have missed this avian drama.

Courtship: Visual and Vocal Displays

Not only is February the season of intensive winter feeding; it is also the season that initiates visual displays in which courtship and breeding accelerate and become highly visible right outside our windows. On a cold morning in late February, a flash of red catches my eye as I walk past the dining room window. I stop and grab the binoculars that I keep close by. A male cardinal, his feathers fluffed against the chill, comes into focus. He is on the ground beneath the feeder. He picks up a black oil sunflower seed in his bill, hops toward the hedge, and stops. I hear the familiar "*chink*" call note as he looks warily in all directions. He hops a few more inches and stops again. Then I hear an answering "*chink*" coming from somewhere inside the hedge. As I scan the shrub with my binoculars I see a female cardinal perched on a limb a short distance from the outer edge of the foliage. Her wings are quivering like those of a baby bird begging for food as she watches the male's every move.

After a moment he flies up into the hedge, utters a piping call, and lands on the sawed-off stub of a limb near the female. He still has the seed in his beak. Soon the two are face to face, and her wings are still aflutter. She opens her mouth and stands waiting. Methodically, the male rotates the seed in his thick bill, cracks it, extracts the nutmeat, and discards the shell. The female tilts her head to one side, and he transfers the tidbit from his bill to hers as gently as lovers exchanging a first kiss. This is a sign of pair bonding. It is like the box of candy or bouquet of flowers among humans. Mate feeding is one of the first visible steps in the breeding cycle of cardinals, and it is not unusual to see this behavior on or near your feeders.

True, only a few weeks earlier I may have seen a little aggressiveness on the part of the male cardinal when both were present in the feeding area. At that time the male made a threatening move toward the female as if attempting to drive her away. At such a time she either moved out of his way or ignored him entirely. It looked as if the honeymoon was over before it started. But such male aggression is typical behavior in mated pairs of cardinals at that time of year. However, once mate feeding begins, the two dine together peacefully throughout the breeding process.

Courtship feeding such as that described between the cardinals is not uncommon among other birds. It has been reported in some forty different families of birds. When you see this type of behavior at your feeder or at woodland edge, you know that courtship between the cardinals has officially begun. Can spring be far behind?

Courtship rituals among the more than nine thousand species of birds in the world range from elaborate to elemental. Cranes, storks, and herons are noted for their complex mating dances, which almost seem choreographed as both sexes come together to perform their graceful ballets. They spread their wings, jump up in the air, and then bow as they call out to one another.

Male Greater and Lesser prairie chickens dance and strut on a traditional breeding ground called a "lek" until a female takes notice and invites one of them to the sidelines for copulation. The Golden Eagle does a fluttering dance high in the sky that ends in a gigantic dive toward its lofty nest. Male terns prance around the shoreline with fish in their beaks or burst into ceremonial flights until a female acknowledges the "good provider" and allows copulation to occur and thus a pair bond to form. Western Grebes dance on the water in their courtship rituals. Mate feeding between the cardinals may not be as showy as some of these rituals, but all these displays, whether elaborate or simple, are means to an end—establishing the pair bond.

Many species of birds are polygamous; however, most are monogamous, at least for a single breeding season if not for life. Many (although not all) ornithologists believe that cardinals mate for life. In other words, a bonded pair of cardinals remains together not only for the breeding season, but for the rest of the year as well. If either mate dies, usually the remaining bird searches for and finds another mate.

How often have you seen at your feeder just one cardinal—a male or a female—in any given season? I daresay your answer is "not often." Usually, when you see one of the pair present, the other is not far away, and you hear their "*chink*" network of communication.

Some ornithologists believe that it is the individual birds' attachment to the nesting site, not their attachment to each other, that brings pairs together year after year. Most bird lovers prefer to believe it is the birds' devotion to each other. But that opinion is considered anthropomorphic and not scientific. Sometimes it is difficult not to be anthropomorphic, especially during what we consider the season of love.

Another sign that spring and breeding season are not far away is the heightened level of countersinging between the pair of cardinals. Often the male sings two or three phrases of a typical cardinal song and then suddenly stops. You may wonder, "Why doesn't he finish his song?" Then, in a few seconds, from somewhere in the distance, you hear the female answer. She matches his song, phrase for phrase, or finishes the song he started—a true Nelson Eddy/Jeanette MacDonald type of duet. This lovely antiphony can go on for hours, with variations in phrasing, and serves as another aid to strengthen their bond.

To me the antiphonal sound, linked with peace at the feeding station, is as welcome as an orchestral overture after a discordant warm-up. It is the signal that the cardinals really mean business. And then those pounds and pounds of black oil sunflower seeds I have provided through the long, cold winter begin to pay off.

For example, I may see a display that Donald and Lillian Stokes describe as the "lopsided-pose," in which one bird of the mated pair raises a wing and spreads the feathers fully, creating a lopsided effect. Or the bird may simply lean to one side without raising the wing. The feathers in the crest are

In an act of pair bonding the male extracts the nutmeat, discards the shell, and transfers the tidbit from his bill to hers.

One courtship ritual that may be described as the "lopsided pose" is usually performed within sight of the mate.

lowered, and the neck and body feathers are sleeked down. The bird rocks back and forth in a swaying fashion, raising first one foot and then the other. The bill is shut during this display, but the bird may utter "*chuck*" calls. The other bird, not more than a few feet away, suddenly joins in this little dance and mimics the first bird's actions. I know of no explanation about why this is done. It merely seems to be a part of the courtship ritual.

Another ceremony incorporates both the visual and the vocal aspects of behavior. It is called "song-flight." The male fluffs out all his breast feathers, raises his crest, sings while flying toward the female, and alights near her. Such flights have been noted ranging in distance from ten to one hundred feet. Occasionally the male directs this song-flight toward a trespassing female in the presence of his mated partner. When this happens the intruding female simply flies away from the displaying male.

Also, a "song-dance" display is entertaining to watch. Several components of the lopsided ritual are evident in this advertisement of sexual prowess, such as shifting the weight of the body from one side to the other; however, in this display the male may change from an erect, upright posture while singing to a bowing posture with bill pointed toward the ground. It is almost like a square-dance routine—"Honor your partner. Do-si-do."

In February and March, defending the territory becomes paramount in the life of the male cardinal. He goes to great lengths to ensure that his block of land is safe from all other intruding males of the species.

On a sunny February morning near Rockport, Texas, Barbara Garland and I stood right at the juncture of the territories of at least four male cardinals. We were surrounded by their territorial proclamations. Every few minutes, one of the males dared to cross over the invisible boundary of another male's territory. Then there ensued a chase reminiscent of the dog-fights of World War II fighter planes. The incumbent male flew after the intruder at breakneck speed, dodging tree limbs with the agility of a swallow in flight. This activity continued until the interloper went back to his own high perch and resumed his territorial song.

Not only does the male cardinal chase away these interlopers, he has been known to attack a piece of red paper or other material or bump against his own reflection in hubcaps, car mirrors, or picture windows and sliding glass doors. This can be quite disruptive to the peaceful life of a homeowner. When the bird sees his image in the shiny surface, he assumes another cardinal is vying for his territory. Often residents are puzzled by this bizarre behavior and think they have a deranged cardinal on their hands when the bird repeatedly bangs his head against the reflection, as if shadowboxing, hour after hour. This relentless battle may persist for days. Occasionally, the female exhibits the same type of behavior. Sometimes it becomes necessary to cover shiny surfaces to restore peace and quiet to the homeowners, to say nothing of trying to keep the bird from harming itself in these near-suicidal attacks.

Another visual display used by the Northern Cardinal as a defense mechanism is described by the Stokeses as "head-forward" behavior. In a situation involving any type of aggression toward another bird, be it an intruding member of the same species or simply a different species jockeying for position at a feeder, the bird crouches with its body in a horizontal position. Its head is thrust forward with crest smoothly lowered, and its mouth may be opened or closed. This is supposed to seem threatening to the other bird.

I have seen this scenario many times at a small tray feeder outside my window. A House Sparrow, for instance, may be eating alone at the feeder, when suddenly a cardinal flies in and lands on the same feeder. When the cardinal goes into this act meant to frighten, with its head thrust forward toward the sparrow, the sparrow departs straightaway and does not return until the cardinal has finished feeding.

These are some of the types of cardinal behavior you may be privileged to observe through your own windows during February and March if you establish a bird sanctuary in your backyard. You provide the food, drink, and shelter, and the birds

In a display of mild aggression the bird lowers its crest and hunches forward.

provide the entertainment. When the stage is set and the curtains are drawn, all the elements that we have come to expect in entertainment are there—sex, violence, tenderness, love triangles, domestic strife, domestic tranquility—and the only charge is the cost of a few pounds of seeds.

Most birds nest in spring and summer . . . because all conditions are then most favorable: warmth, full foliage for hiding nests, abundance of food, long days for gathering it for their young.

—Alexander F. Skutch

Infancy, we say, is hedged about by many perils; but the infancy of birds is cradled and pillowed in peril.

—John Burroughs

April through July:
Nesting and Breeding Season

*B*iology professor Fred Gehlbach examined eight eastern and central North American suburban breeding bird censuses (Ohio, Ontario, Kansas, Massachusetts, New Jersey, North Carolina, Texas, Washington, D.C.) and found the Northern Cardinal to be the seventh most widespread and frequent nesting species. It fell behind the European Starling, American Robin, House Sparrow, Blue Jay, Common Grackle, and Song Sparrow. In his study plot in Columbus, Ohio, however, the cardinal ranked sixth, and at Waco, Texas, third.

In the Deep South, nesting sometimes begins in February, but in most parts of the country, Northern Cardinals begin building their nests in early April. In the more northern areas of the cardinal's range, nesting may begin considerably later. Cardinals, like most other songbirds, build complex cupped nests in which to lay their eggs and raise their young, and they use a variety of places and a diversity of vegetation.

From the human's point of view, the name of the avian game seems to be concealment since nests are fairly hard to locate. The fact is, we don't *know* whether birds deliberately set out to place their nests where they will be hidden or not.

How do cardinals go about deciding where to build their nests? The process of site selection is almost always basically the same, step by step, and may be illustrated by a scenario that took place several times over a period of two years only inches from the window of my study. The first time I observed the action in the nandina bush, a male cardinal hopped slowly and deliberately from one branch to another, saying *"chink"* from time to time as he seemed to examine the configuration of the branches. He lingered awhile in the section next to the window screen then hopped to the outer edge of the bush and looked toward the neighbor's house where I saw the female cardinal perched in a shrub watching him. After repeating *"chink"* a few more times, he sang a brief song and flew over to her.

Soon the female came to the bush to look around. She explored the same branches the male had examined, and he joined her there. She crouched in one spot for a few minutes as if sitting on a nest. The male came to her side and sat very close to her. "*Chinks*" flew back and forth between them faster than a tennis ball at Wimbledon. I began to suspect they were looking for a nesting site.

Advantages and disadvantages of using this particular bush were clearly apparent to me, and probably to the birds as well. At first it seemed an almost ideal location as far as shelter was concerned. Here, with thick overhanging leaves, they would be protected from sun and rain. Moreover, the bush was only fifteen yards from the sunflower feeder in my backyard, which would provide a convenient food supply.

The major disadvantage that I recognized was the large cat that had raided the mockingbird's nest one week before in a holly bush just six feet away. Of course, I have no idea whether the cat was a factor, but, for whatever reasons, the pair did not begin transporting nest materials to the bush as I had hoped they would.

Nevertheless, so goes the selective process of cardinals looking for the best location for a nest. The intervals of searching increase in length daily as the nest-building drive matures. The pair may spend several days going from site to site within their territory, searching, as these two did outside my window, until they find a satisfactory location. Over the next several days, the scenario was repeated in the same bush at least three times by the birds that year. And the same thing happened the following spring. Each time my expectations rose to a higher level; each time there was a disappointing ending after a promising buildup. I suppose it was too much to ask for a pair of cardinals to nest right outside my window while this book was in preparation.

Cardinals nest in a surprising assortment of vegetation and places. Despite the intensity of the nest site search, cardinals make their homes sometimes in precarious places with life-and-death consequences. When Barbara Garland was searching for nests to photograph for this book, she at first found six. The first, in a suburban area, was in a mock orange tree 5½ feet from the ground. After the eggs had been hatched only a few days, a neighborhood dog destroyed both nest and nestlings.

The second was in a huge blackjack oak tree with long spreading limbs that almost touched the ground. This nest, at the end of one of the low-hanging limbs, was only four feet off the ground. One morning the homeowners at this rural location watched in horror as a snake ate all four eggs that were in the nest. Cardinals are known for this seemingly careless, close-to-the-ground nest site selection, which seems odd to us after such a long search.

A boxwood hedge provided concealment for the third nest Barbara found. It was located next to a friend's house and about six feet from the ground. After sitting on two eggs for a few days, the female cardinal inexplicably abandoned the nest.

Barbara was beginning to think she would never find a successful nest. However, this type of destruction and disruption is really not unusual. Gehlbach's notes reveal that in his suburban study area long-term nesting success was 39 percent. That means a little more than one of every three nesting attempts was successful. In a rural study plot, he found success at 17 percent—less than one nest in five. Gehlbach concluded that these differences are statistically significant and in keeping with what is known about urban versus rural populations of a species in a particular geographic area—namely, the urban population is more successful, largely because of decreased predation.

Just when Barbara thought all was lost, a friend called and told her about a cardinal nest located in a waxleaf ligustrum adjacent to her home. The female cardinal on this nest succeeded in raising three young.

The fifth nest was in a topiary hedge. From a clutch of four eggs, only one nestling survived to leave the nest. The sixth nest was found barely clinging to the stalks of some dead bamboo shoots. Surprisingly, three babies fledged from this precarious site.

A nest in Toronto was found only two or three feet from one of the busiest walkways in High Park. Hundreds of people daily passed within arm's reach of the cardinal's nest, which was situated three feet from the ground in an Austrian pine. Another nest was found in a vine growing on the side wall of someone's back porch directly under the kitchen window and three or four feet from a door through which people passed in and out all day.

My son's family witnessed a cardinal family thrive nestled in a hanging basket of boxwood fern inside a covered patio that was enclosed on three sides. The parent birds flew through the open end of the patio to attend their nesting duties. The next spring, after my son had placed screenwire across the open end of the patio, he saw a female cardinal hitting against the screen. Because the hanging basket was still in the same place, the family wondered if the same bird was attempting to nest there again.

I once found a cardinal building her nest in a Virginia creeper vine that clings to the screen on one of my bedroom windows. Arthur Cleveland Bent reports a nest built in a small bush inside a greenhouse connected to a flower shop in the center of a city. The birds gained entrance through a broken window pane that the owner obligingly put off repairing until after the young had fledged.

My friend Floyce Moon, a retired school teacher, told me of a cardinal pair who built their nest in a pyracantha bush about three feet outside one of her classroom windows. When her students were at the reading table they had ringside seats to all the activities, including nest building, incubation of the eggs, and feeding of the young. One Friday the nestlings began to hop onto the edge of the nest, and by Monday morning the nest was empty. When the first-graders arrived at school that morning, they were very disappointed that they had missed seeing the fledglings when they left the nest. But their disappointment abated later that day when they saw the whole cardinal family touring the area. It appeared that the young birds were being given a crash course on survival for the next several days. My friend knew the experience made a lasting impression on her students, because at the close of the school year the children wrote notes about what they had liked best about first grade. Nearly all of them named "the redbirds."

In 1944 Amelia R. Laskey studied 103 cardinal nests near Nashville, Tennessee. She reported: "As nest sites, cardinals choose young evergreens of many varieties; privet hedges; many species of vines, including rose and honeysuckle; shrubbery; and saplings of hackberry, elm, hawthorn, and locust." She said one cardinal built a nest on a platform of twigs that she personally placed in a privet shrub where the birds had tried unsuccessfully to anchor nesting materials.

In the Everglades, cardinals may nest in bushes along the banks of the canals. In other parts of Florida, nests are found in palmetto or oak bushes, in small orange trees, in clumps of vines, or saddled on the limbs of mango trees. In Arizona and other areas in the Southwest you may see cardinals nesting in mesquite trees. In Mississippi they are found in orchards and the thickest of canebrakes among a variety of other places. In Central Texas one may find them in dense shrubs, especially coralberry and deciduous holly, in vine tangles of greenbrier, and in shrubby eastern red cedar trees.

In the southern Alleghenies cardinals prefer the edges of brooks, rocky slopes, and dense ravines where azaleas, rhododendrons, mountain laurels, and many other sweet-scented shrubs form dense and extensive thickets. In southwestern Missouri, Henry Nehrling found cardinals nesting in snowberry, wild rose, and gooseberry bushes. In southern Louisiana he found them in the undergrowth on the edges of cypress swamps. All over the South he discovered numerous nests in the beautiful dense hedges of Cherokee rose.

Cardinals rarely build their nests in the open. Surprisingly, Gehlbach found a successful one in a lone four-foot shrub by a window, bordered on the outside by a concrete driveway. Laskey reports a cardinal nest on the ledge of a lattice fence between pieces of poultry wire with nothing for concealment. Another rare nest site was on a feeding shelf outside a second-story window. One of the most bizarre cardinal nest sites was in a woven-wire sparrow trap on a beam fifteen feet above the floor in an outbuilding. The cardinals successfully nested there in two different seasons.

This wide variety makes it quite evident that cardinals are not averse to living near habitations and they show no marked preference as to the kind of vegetation in which they nest, apart from a strong affinity for dense understory.

From all these descriptions it seems that cardinals prefer to nest at fairly low levels. Their nests are generally placed between three and twenty feet from the ground, more often below ten feet. A nest placed more than twenty feet high is rare but not unheard of. On a river bank in a flooded area, Barbara found a cardinal nest thirty feet high in an elm tree.

Nest sizes among birds generally vary according to the size of the bird. Not surprisingly, hummingbirds make the smallest ones. The Ruby-throated Hummingbird's nest is no bigger than a demitasse—about an inch deep and an inch across. The largest tree nests of birds in North America are those of the Bald Eagle. One measured 20 feet deep and 9½ feet across. A cardinal's nest would seem dwarfed if placed alongside one of such gargantuan proportions. The cupped nest of the Northern Cardinal has a depth of 1⅝ inches, a height of 3¼ inches, and an outside diameter of 5⅜ inches.

There is wide diversity in the kinds of nests constructed by different birds—from the floating nests of grebes and coots to the large platforms of sticks used by Ospreys and the simple scrapes on bare ground used by gulls, terns, and many other shorebirds. Most of the songbirds, including cardinals, build open cuplike nests.

In some species of the world's birds, both male and female assist in assembling the nest. In other species, only one partner participates. In shrikes the male builds the nest alone. In hummingbirds, the male never even sees the nest. In the case of the Northern Cardinal, the female does most of the construction herself, but the male is never far away. Many times he helps his mate in gathering building materials and occasionally assists in their placement.

Once the site selection is made, a pair of cardinals will cruise their territory searching for all the "right stuff" that goes into the nest. The female usually leads as the two fly across an open area. One or both may have nesting materials in their beaks. A good way to find a cardinal nest is to follow the female when you see her repeatedly going into the same thicket or shrub, but be very careful not to disturb. Human curiosity is often due cause for a bird to build a new nest in a different location. So, if you must watch, do so from a safe distance.

Just what is the "right stuff" for cardinal nests? Naturally, it depends on the part of the country in which you look. In some localities you might find grasses and fine rootlets, old leaves, horse hair, pine needles, twigs, grapevine bark, weed stems, rags, forb stalks, strips of paper, and other debris. In a nest found in a ravine in Central Texas, the major component was red cedar bark strips. A cardinal nest in the swamps of Louisiana may be composed almost entirely of Spanish moss and grasses and decorated with a snake skin around the rim. A nest in Tamaulipas, Mexico, may contain a large amount of goat's hair in the lining.

A third-grader once called me and said her class was studying birds, and her assignment was to build a nest like a cardinal's. She asked my advice on how to go about it. Even though I had watched cardinals building a nest I was hard put to give her an answer. An old French proverb says that humans can do everything except build a bird's nest. If you've ever watched the nest building process, undoubtedly you will agree. I once observed a hummingbird daily from the time it attached a small platform on a down-sloping branch of a pecan tree until it decorated the outside of the finished structure with tiny bits of lichen which it stuck in place with its own saliva. I've never seen a human-made form to equal it.

It is amazing to think that the only tools most birds use are their bills and feet, and yet they are able to weave complex structures that stand up to the worst of adversities and look like works of art. Doubtless, few humans are capable of building a house using only their mouths and feet as tools. Since a bird's bill is primarily adapted for eating or food gathering, one might suppose the avian architect has difficulty in using the same tool for building purposes. Most birds, though, seem adept at making this adjustment, and the cardinal is no exception. It uses its short, stout seed-cracking bill quite efficiently when it comes time to fetch, place, and organize the materials it chooses for its nest. Likewise, its feet, used primarily for perching, skillfully come into play for pushing, lifting, and arranging the building supplies required for the inside layer of the cuplike receptacle.

The actual process of building the nest is roughly divided into three steps: preparing the site or support, constructing the floor and sides, and lining the nest. A cardinal nest has four distinct layers. The first layer, or foundation, is a platform of stiff weed stems or small sticks that the female carefully places in the selected site. Incidentally, the bird who builds in a bush must know just what configuration of branches is needed to provide adequate support for the nest. That is one reason it takes considerable time to find just the right place. No doubt this knowledge is gained through trial and error.

The second layer is of softer, more pliable materials, such as old leaves, strips of various kinds of bark, pieces of paper, or grass. This layer forms the outside walls of the cupped nest. Some cardinal nests I have examined are really sloppy, having loose strands of paper hanging out all around them.

The third layer consists of finer weeds and grasses and trailing vines. During the process of completing this layer, the female sits in the middle of the cup that is taking shape, and pulls long slender pieces of plant fiber, one at a time with her bill, inward over the rim. She tucks each of these into the wall under her breast or alongside her body. She squats inside the nest and presses—with her head, her feet, her wings, her tail, or her whole body—against the rim of the cup. Rotating her body, she repeats these actions each time she brings new materials to the site, thus forming a round nest. Next she loops a similar bit of fiber around a supporting branch and secures the end of it inside the wall of the nest. She repeats this step until the structure is securely tied to several supporting branches.

The fourth, and final, layer is the softest. It is the lining where she lays the eggs—the equivalent of the receiving blanket in the nursery where the young will be nurtured. It contains fine rootlets, pine needles, horse hair, goat hair, dog hair, human hair, or Spanish moss—anything soft that is available. When forming this layer, she nestles as low as she can inside the concavity and squirms about until the fit is perfect and there is plenty of room underneath her for the eggs.

During the nesting season, it is fun to place strands of yarn or clumps of hair in a bush or tree and watch for the cardinals and other birds to find them. It usually does not take the birds long to discover the treasures.

Even with all the complicated weaving, squirming, poking, and pushing, the female cardinal still ends up with a rather frail and loose structure. If you could examine a nest closely, you might wonder how the parent birds ever succeed in bringing up young in such a receptacle.

The length of time required to build a nest varies with weather conditions, availability of supplies, and with the species. Some birds spend months on nest construction. Greater Thornbirds of Paraguay may work all winter on their huge stick nests. Bushtits take up to fifty days on their foot-long hanging pocket nests. The Ruby-throated Hummingbird I watched spent five days completing hers, and I do not know how long she had been working before I discovered it. A Golden Eagle may take up to two months, and Northern Orioles ten to twelve days.

Recorded lengths of time for cardinals to complete their nests range from three to nine days. Thus cardinals are on the lower end of the scale of time spent on construction. Moreover, birds do not work constantly, all day long, nor every day. They usually work for a few hours early in the morning and a few hours late in the evening until the nest is complete. And, just as construction crews sometimes have to postpone outside work if inclement weather occurs, so may cardinals delay their work for a day or two until conditions improve.

Birds expend a tremendous amount of energy in the process of nest building. Barn Swallows make more than 1,200 trips to collect the mud needed for only one nest. A Black-throated Oriole's nest in Mexico was found to contain 3,387 separate pieces of grass and plant fibers. I don't know how many items go into a cardinal nest, but on a museum specimen of a hummingbird's nest I counted over 250 bits of lichen, and that was just the decoration on the outside walls. In a House Sparrow's nest near Chapel Hill, North Carolina, John K. Terres reported 1,282 items. The list included mostly grasses and some strips of grapevine bark, but it also included part of an envelope postmarked "New York 17" and, appropriately, a piece of a letter bearing the typed words "difficult struggle."

In most birds, copulation occurs intermittently during the period between pair bonding and egg laying and sometimes continues through incubation and care of the young. This is true especially in those birds that raise more than one brood as do the cardinals. Although in most cases the male is the aggressor, the female often invites coition by song, call note, a particular posture, or a provocative display. The song of the female cardinal seems to be one of the strongest stimuli for the male.

Donald and Lillian Stokes report that it is not all that common to observe cardinals in the act of mating. Robert E. Lemon found this to be true in his study of cardinals in Ontario: "Actual copulation was noted only a few times in the wild and then only from some distance."

While Barbara Garland was photographing cardinals for this book she observed cardinals mating on three different occasions. She said the first time she saw a pair mate, the female was perched perpendicular to a branch with her wings lowered and quivering while she awaited the male's approach. When he appeared his crest was erect and he looked really alert. When he got close to the female, she crouched down with her beak and tail pointed upward and her breast feathers fluffed. She spread her tail to one side so that her vent (cloacal opening) was exposed. The male sidled down the limb to her, mounted her back, touched her vent with his, and thus transmitted the sperm from his body to hers. It was over almost in the blinking of an eye—too fast for Barbara even to focus the camera.

Barbara's second observation of coition between cardinals was the pair who each had only one foot. Not surprisingly, these two mated on the ground, solving their balancing problems. The third time she observed mating, the cardinals had just finished feeding nestlings. This time coition occurred on the rim of the nest, and although Barbara was ready for the action with her camera, her flash failed to perform.

The Values of Summer Feeding throughout Egg Laying, Incubation, and Care of the Young

The interval between completion of the nest and laying of the first egg varies among species as well as among individual birds. With cardinals egg laying usually begins up to six days after the nest is finished. After expending so much effort on gathering building supplies and actually constructing the nest, most female birds take time to rest and renew their energy before laying their eggs. This is one reason it is important to continue feeding the birds through the breeding season even though natural foods are in abundance at this time. Birds will readily take the supplemental nourishment you provide for their myriad calorie-consuming activities connected with breeding. Additionally, an accessible food supply may encourage the birds to nest in your garden.

The following are some suggestions of items you can easily provide for this critical time in the life of your favorite redbirds:

1. Finely crushed eggshells provide females with added calcium vital to the development of eggs in their own bodies. These can be offered in the feeder right along with sunflower seeds.

2. A peanut butter mixture for summertime feeding to take the place of the suet mixture mentioned earlier for the winter months is designed not to become rancid in summer heat. Mix together in a bowl: one part peanut butter, four parts cornmeal, one part flour, and one part vegetable shortening. No cooking is necessary. This can be offered in the same sort of feeder as earlier suggested for the suet mix—a hanging log with perches. Store any excess in the refrigerator.

3. Mealworms are another source of vital nutrients to offer at summer feeding stations. They are readily eaten by cardinals, and the adults often feed them to their young. As previously suggested, buy mealworms at a bait shop or pet store, or ask a biology teacher for a supply catalog.

After a few days of rest, it is time for the female to get on with her task of egg laying. Once the male's sperm cells enter her body they swim to the upper end of the oviduct, where one fertilizes the ovum (yolk) before the shell forms around it. Thus begins the development of an embryo.

The ovum goes through several stages as it passes through the reproductive tract of the female. At one stage the egg white (albumen) forms. Next the inner and outer shell membranes are formed. Then the ovum moves into the uterus, where it remains for a little over twenty hours. At this stage, during the last five hours before the egg is actually laid, the hard outer shell is formed and colored with pigments.

There is an almost infinite variety in the colors and markings of bird eggs. Even within a species, eggs can be remarkably diverse, sometimes making it difficult for a novice to determine the kind of bird that laid them. Some birds produce eggs that are uniformly colored. For example, a woodpecker's eggs are pure white, highly glossy, and look like the finest of translucent porcelains. Robins' and bluebirds' eggs are light blue. The Great Tinamou of the tropical American forests lays eggs that are intense turquoise blue with a high gloss.

Most birds, however, produce eggs with some combination of ground color and various markings. These markings may be in the form of blotches, scrawls, streaks, marbling, or speckles. Northern Cardinal eggs follow this pattern. Usually the largest concentration of color forms a wreath around the large end of the egg, since it passes first through the major supply of pigments from the cellular walls of the bird's birth canal.

Egg size varies among species almost as much as color. The egg of one of the smallest hummingbirds is one-half inch in length by one-quarter inch in thickness and weighs about 0.3 grams. An ostrich egg, on the opposite end of the scale, is six inches by five inches and weighs 1,600 grams. Between these two extremes we find the cardinal's egg, which is about one inch long and weighs around 8.6 grams. Thus the ostrich egg weighs 5,333 times as much as the hummer's and 186 times as much as the cardinal's.

Most songbirds lay their eggs very early in the morning. When the time is right for the female cardinal, she enters the nest before daylight or the evening before. Once the egg is complete inside her body, it passes quickly through the muscular cloaca. During the next stage, the bird may rise from time to time and look beneath her to see if anything is happening. After one to three minutes of bearing down, the female expels her first egg, blunt end first, through the cloaca.

Approximately twenty-four hours later the entire process is repeated and a second egg appears in the nest. This goes on daily until the clutch is complete. A clutch is the total number of eggs laid in an uninterrupted series, for a single nesting, by one female. This is not to be confused with the total number of eggs found in a given nest, as various circumstances may affect the final count. For example, predators may remove or eat some of the eggs, or other birds may lay their eggs in the cardinal's nest, as we shall see later.

Occasionally two females of the same species lay their eggs in one nest and then share incubation duties. Oscar Hawksley and Alvah P. McCormack found a nest on which two female cardinals were actually incubating at the same time facing in opposite directions. In Topeka, Kansas, a partially albino cardinal and a normally colored one shared a nest. Together they incubated five eggs that were apparently the product of both females fertilized by one male—an exception to monogamy. When the young hatched, all three adult birds shared in feeding the five nestlings.

There is at least one instance on record when joint nesting efforts were undertaken by birds of two genera. Mr. and Mrs. George Swinford, of Erlanger, Kentucky, were surprised to find pairs of Northern Cardinals and American Robins sharing the same nest in a forsythia bush beside their porch. Karl Maslowski, a professional nature photographer and writer, was called upon to document the unusual occurrence on film. He reported that the nest construction was definitely a community effort, because the bottom half was typical of most cardinal nests and the top half was a robin's stick-and-mud bowl lined with grass.

When Maslowski first examined the nest he found four robin nestlings, two cardinals, and one unhatched cardinal egg. He observed that the females of both species shared brooding responsibilities, and both males assisted in feeding the babies. He reported that when the nestlings were young, the adult birds cross-fed all of them, but when they were about one week old, the parents began to feed only their own offspring. All the young of this unusual nesting co-op were raised to fledgling stage.

For now, consider normal the cardinal's clutch of two to five eggs, three to four being most common. The eggs are typically oval—sometimes long-oval, sometimes short-oval—with an overall measurement of 25.3 millimeters by 18.2 millimeters (about one inch long), and they weigh about 8.6 grams. They are smooth and semiglossy with a background color of white or slightly greenish, speckled and spotted in various degrees with small blotches of brown and reddish brown to pale purple and gray. As a rule, the heaviest spotting is concentrated on the larger end of the egg. However, sometimes the egg's surface is so heavily blotched that the background color is almost totally obscured.

Shortly after the egg is laid, a small air pocket forms at the large end between the two membranes that rest against the inside wall of the shell. As the embryo develops, water evaporates from the egg and the air chamber grows larger. A few hours before hatching, the embryo shifts positions and the head and bill come in contact with the membrane, which is then pierced. The baby cardinal begins to breathe this unique oxygen supply in preparation for its debut into the outside world.

Among cardinals, incubation at full intensity doesn't begin until after the last egg of the clutch is laid. Incubation is the act of a parent bird sitting on its eggs and applying body heat. Maintaining a constant temperature is vital to the rapid development of the embryos and the ultimate hatching of the chicks.

In order to accomplish this transfer of heat from the incubating bird to the eggs, most songbirds develop what is called an incubation patch—a small area on the abdomen from which the down feathers are dropped a few days before the eggs are to be laid. The blood vessels in this exposed area become enlarged and increase in number so that the skin thickens and becomes swollen. This heavy concentration of blood vessels near the surface provides a constant source of heat, roughly 104 degrees Fahrenheit. This special patch lasts for the duration of the breeding season whether only one brood or three to four are raised. The feathers on the abdomen are replaced during the fall molt, but until then, the incubating and brooding bird has a built-in heating pad.

When the female cardinal enters the nest to begin incubation, she carefully wiggles her body around until she can best cover the eggs. She fluffs her breast feathers so that the incubation patch is exposed and settles down on the eggs. Periodically she raises herself, turns the eggs with her bill, and then gently settles again in the nest, possibly facing in another direction.

During the application of this special heating pad, the embryo inside the tiny eggshell undergoes dramatic changes. A time-lapse photography sequence of what is occurring inside an egg would show that first the number of cells increases. When large enough numbers have formed, one of the most miraculous processes of life begins. Groups of cells move about and rearrange themselves, and through ensuing days the head, eyes, heart, and blood vessels start to form. In a surprisingly short time, a baby bird takes shape inside its protective covering of porous shell, which allows the transfer of oxygen and gaseous waste. While all this is happening, the yolk inside provides nutrition vital to the life of a healthy nestling, since there is no umbilical cord linking the embryo to its mother.

Generally speaking, in those species in which the sexes are outwardly alike, the male and female share equally in incubation of the eggs. The Killdeer is a familiar example of this pattern. Among phalaropes the male takes full responsibility for incubation and care of the young. However, with most passerines (songbirds) it is usually the duller-colored female, as in cardinals, that plays the major role in incubation. Supposedly, her dull color provides camouflage that protects her and the nestlings from detection by predators; but occasionally the crimson male cardinal will relieve his mate of these duties for short periods of time.

During the days the eggs are being incubated, the female seldom leaves the nest for long periods. Naturally she has to devote some time to her own health with short forays for feeding,

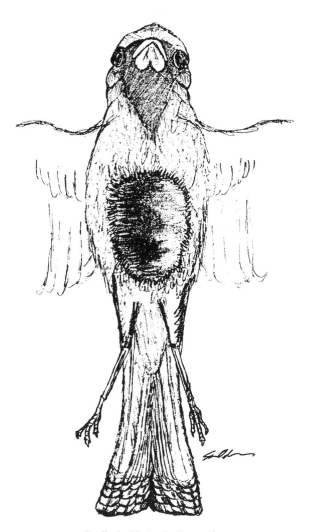

Cardinal with incubation patch.
Drawing by Sam Osborne.

bathing, and preening, but these jaunts are never lengthy. Throughout this critical time the male is very attentive to the female. He often sings near the nest, and once in awhile the female is heard answering his song with a soft one of her own from the nest. Or he may warn her with alarm notes if danger is near. Several times a day he brings food and feeds her in the same fashion as during their courtship period. This not only helps keep up her strength for the long days and hours of sitting; it also helps to strengthen the birds' attachment to each other. Often these visits end in coition, resulting in another brood.

Departure from and return to the nest by both birds of the pair follow the same pattern. When leaving the slightly elevated nest, the bird departs quickly in a downward direction and flies away at a low level to take advantage of the dense understory that usually surrounds the nest site. The procedure is reversed for the return to the nest. This extra caution is yet another deterrent to predators.

The time involved in incubation varies greatly among the species. Generally, those that produce well-developed (precocial) chicks take longer to incubate, and those with helpless (altricial) nestlings take a shorter time. Experts have found no incubation period shorter than eleven days. The Brown-headed Cowbird hatches after eleven days of incubation, which is definitely to the cowbird's advantage as we shall see later.

The Northern Cardinal's incubation period is usually twelve to thirteen days. When the baby bird is almost ready to hatch, it develops a strong "hatching muscle" and an egg tooth—a short, pointed calcareous structure on the tip of the upper half of its bill. Toward the end of the twelve to thirteen days, the fully developed embryo, with the help of its hatching muscle, rubs and scrapes its egg tooth against the walls of the shell, which have weakened because of loss of mineral substances that have dissolved out of the shell. The scraping continues until a small star-shaped puncture appears. This process is called *pipping*. During the next several hours the embryo pushes with its head and feet, alternately struggling and resting, until the cracks radiate around the larger end of the egg. When the cracks have weakened the shell sufficiently, the nestling works its way out, and a new life finds itself in daylight. The cardinal parents then either eat the eggshells or carry them some distance away from the nest to prevent betraying the nest's location to predators.

The first calls that baby cardinals make are faint sounds given at the time of hatching. By the time they leave the nest, nine to eleven days later, they give a variety of food-begging calls, which are slurred up or down.

One could hardly describe the newly hatched cardinal as "cute." It is an ungainly bundle of skin and bones—thin pink skin tightly drawn over a tiny skeleton and sparsely covered with mouse-gray natal down. It has bulging eyes covered with dark lids, a wobbly head, a swollen abdomen grotesquely disproportionate to the rest of its body, short undeveloped legs and wings, a large gaping mouth lined with bright red to make an easy target when being fed, and yellowish-white flanges (projecting folds of skin) outlining the red chasm that seems a bottomless pit. This is indeed a sight that only a mother bird could love. Within a week after hatching, the nestling's egg tooth gradually disappears without apparently falling off.

All birds are altricial or precocial at hatching. *Altricial* comes from the Latin word meaning "nurse." Helpless altricial youngsters require as much care as a human infant, and some believe that altricials are born prematurely. *Precocial,* the opposite of *altricial,* stems from the Latin word *Praecox,* "to ripen beforehand." The young chicks are able to move about shortly after hatching and require little or no parental care. They are born with their eyes wide open and are covered in down, a semblance of adult plumage. They leave the nest as soon as they are dry. Cardinals are altricial and thus require immediate care from their parents.

For awhile, cardinal nestlings are cold-blooded and unable to regulate their body temperature on their own. Since no bird has perfected a method for warming its young other than with its own body, the brooding parent must continue behavior similar to incubation and provide the necessary heat. Here again, that built-in heating pad comes in handy. Should the parent have to leave the nest for an extended period, the nestling's temperature drops or rises to the level of the surrounding air. In most cases this is not lethal unless the temperature is excessively low or excessively high. Excessive heat tends to be more of a threat to the life of a nestling than is cold. The brood-

Once the nest site is selected, the cardinals cruise their territory in search of "all the right stuff."

ing parent protects the young from sun and rain by covering the entire nest with outstretched wings like an umbrella. At about midpoint in nest life, the nestling attains body temperature control and no longer has to be brooded by the parent.

The newly hatched cardinal sprawls in the nest, too weak to hold up its head. It rests on its abdomen, its head slightly under its breast and its legs thrust forward. Early activities consist mainly of feeding, defecating, and sleeping. For a few hours after breaking out of the shell, the bird receives nourishment from the egg yolk which it absorbed in its stomach shortly before hatching. When that supply is depleted, the nestling lifts its wobbly head straight up, opens its mouth in a wide gape, and starts begging for food. The begging actions of the young, their yellowish flanges, and their bright red mouth lining all provide stimuli for the adult birds to begin feeding.

The next few days are frantically busy for both parents as they work to fill the gaping mouths of their three or four fast-growing, hungry nestlings. At a cardinal nest reported by A. C. Bent, over a period of 6½ hours the two young were fed 178 times, an average of 89 times each. The longest interval he noted between feeding visits was thirty-five minutes, and the shortest was two minutes.

The nestling's main diet for the first few days of life consists of insects—moths, bugs, larvae of various kinds, and green caterpillars and then later grasshoppers and beetles. W. L. McAtee noted that 94.75 percent of their food was found to be animal matter and 5.25 percent vegetable. The proportions of the principal food items of the nestlings he studied were as follows: cicadas, 17.25 percent; grasshoppers, 20 percent; caterpillars, 21.25 percent; and beetles, 23.25 percent. The vegetable matter consisted of corn, rice, kafir corn, oats, and wheat, all of which made up only 8.73 percent of the total food, and much of this was waste grain. He also listed thirty-three species of wild fruits that are occasionally fed to nestlings. The parents collect the food, return to the nest, turn their heads sideways, poke their beaks into the gullets of the nestlings to stimulate the swallowing reflex, and finally regurgitate the food deep into the young birds' throats.

The urge to feed is a very strong instinct in birds, sometimes even in those that are just beginning to nest. For example, some parent birds have been observed attempting to give food to the eggs. Once a young cardinal was placed in the nest of a Bell's Vireo just after the last egg of its clutch was laid. The vireo immediately began feeding the baby cardinal.

Sometimes the urge to feed transcends species and even class boundaries. A Northern Cardinal was observed in Shelby, North Carolina, feeding a group of goldfish in a pond. Perhaps the cardinal had lost its brood to predators, and when it went to the pond to drink, it saw the gaping mouths of the goldfish and couldn't resist the urge to feed them. For several days the cardinal expertly delivered mouthful after mouthful of worms to the hungry fish.

One might suppose that the parents feed their young by turns in rotation, but this is not the case. The hungriest gets fed first and continues to be fed until it is satisfied, then the next hungriest, and so on until all are fed. It seems to be a contest: whichever nestling raises its head the highest with its mouth wide open is first to be fed. When that nestling has had enough it ceases to swallow the food placed in its throat. The parent then lifts the unswallowed food from that nestling's throat and places it in the next highest open beak it sees. Alexander Skutch found that small songbirds are fed an average of four to twelve meals per hour per nestling. If those numbers hold true for a cardinal brood of four, the parents might make up to forty-eight trips per hour to feed their young. For nearly all species, the rate of feeding increases the longer the young are in the nest.

With that kind of service from attentive parents, the nestlings soon take on a growing spurt that is unequaled in the world of mammals. At the time of hatching, the weight of most passerine nestlings is equal to about two-thirds the weight of the fresh egg, or 6 to 8 percent of the weight of the adult female. When they are ready to leave the nest, at nine to eleven days of age, they weigh about 70 to 80 percent of the weight of the female parent.

In her study of Song Sparrows, Margaret Morse Nice notes

Both parents work diligently to feed their hungry nestlings.

that the first four days of nest life are characterized by rapid growth, the start of feather development, the food response, and defecation. This serves as a guide to the development of young cardinals as well. Days five and six are days of rapid weight gain, the establishment of temperature control, and a virtual explosion of feathers. Blue-sheathed feathers erupt as if in the hands of a magician. First they sprout as spiky quills; then they quickly grow and expand until the body is well covered. Sometime during these two days the nestling opens its eyes and begins standing, stretching its legs, and conducting rudimentary preening activities.

On days seven, eight, and nine, motor skill development is even more rapid. The nestlings begin to stretch and fan their wings, and they flutter them when begging for food. By the time the young leave the nest, they have lost their natal down and are covered by juvenal plumage. They are now fledglings.

In addition to feeding the young to spur their rapid growth, parent birds must keep the nest sanitary. Adult birds carry something away from the nest after almost every feeding episode. This is the fecal sac—a tough mucous membrane enclosing the feces of young nestlings. In cardinals this sac resembles a miniature disposable diaper. The high content of uric acid makes it white, and it looks like a small package neatly wrapped in white plastic.

Since the digestive tract of a nestling is far from perfect, each episode of feeding stimulates defecation. Usually the parent that brings food to the young waits on the side of the nest while the baby digests its food. After the nestling eats, it falls forward in the nest, exposes its vent, and defecates. The parent then reaches into the nest with its bill and removes the fecal sac, sometimes lifting it directly from the vent. Cardinal parents have been observed to eat the sac for four or five days after the nestlings hatch. This conservation measure makes use of the undigested food. Beginning about the fifth or sixth day the parents fly away from the nest before disposing of the sac so as not to reveal the nest's location to predators.

Defending the young in the nest from predators is another activity that consumes time and energy of the parent birds.

Cardinals have numerous enemies—raccoons, snakes, rats, cats, dogs, and, of course, other birds, such as hawks, crows, and owls.

Small birds have been observed dive-bombing cats and dogs and even people who came too close to their nests or young. Mockingbirds and Blue Jays are notorious for this behavior. During the nesting season I often receive phone calls from nervous homeowners who say they are being attacked by an angry bird every time they try to leave their homes. I explain to them that the bird is simply trying to defend its young from harm.

I also get calls from people asking the same question time and time again: "When a baby bird falls from a nest, if I pick it up and put it back, will the parents have anything more to do with the baby?" The answer is, "Yes, they will." An old wives' tale promotes the belief that once human hands touch a nestling or an egg, the parent birds will no longer care for that bird or egg. This is not true. It is just a myth. The human scent will not curtail the parents' responsibilities at the nest. What it may do, however, is attract predators to the nest. The lesson here is to think twice before you try to give human assistance in such an instance. Infancy of birds is, indeed, "cradled and pillowed in peril" from many quarters.

The Fledgling

Birds face many adversities while their young are still in the nest. It is a wonder that any survive to become fledglings, but survive they do. When the youngsters are ready to leave the nest the cardinal family may put on quite a show. A friend of mine called one day to invite me to the "coming-out party" of a group of three young cardinals that were ready to fledge from a nest in a hanging basket on her patio.

When I arrived on the scene one fledgling was perched on the rim of the nest, another was on the wooden fence a few feet away from the basket, and the third was on the ground eight or ten feet away from the parents. The parents were vociferous in their efforts at encouraging the three. Loud "*chinks*" were coming from both parties. One or the other of the parents took a few steps toward the fledgling on the ground, uttered several insistent "*chinks*," then turned and hopped away from it. If the baby refused to move, the adult repeated the procedure until the youngster made an effort to come toward the parent. After several moments of urging, the fledgling spread its tiny wings and feebly flew to a tree, where it alighted several feet from the ground.

After that accomplishment the parents concentrated on the "fence" bird. "*Chink! Chink! Chink!*" the parents called repeatedly. The fledgling finally made the long flight from the top of the fence to the ground. Each time one of the young made an advance, the parents appeared to praise it with lavish "*chinks*." Finally, all three of the young were out of the nest. The parents then led the fledglings into a thicket and out of our sight.

During the early days of fledglinghood, the parents go to great efforts to keep the young out of harm's way. Hiding them in a thicket until they are capable fliers is one method they use to protect the brood. I never see young that are right out of the nest at my feeders. It is usually after the young have reached almost adult size that family groups begin to forage together.

The fledgling stage is defined as the period between the time the bird leaves the nest and the time when it becomes completely independent of parental care. Here again, the period is characterized by dramatic changes and rapid growth. It would be interesting if one could follow the family just described for the next three weeks, the normal length of time young are dependent upon the adults. During this period, the male parent continues to oversee care of the brood if they are the first of the season, teaching them survival skills that will help protect them for the rest of their lives. While this is happening, the female builds another nest and starts another brood. If it is the final brood of the season, both parents share equally in the care of the young until they are independent.

Texas naturalist Roy Bedichek told an interesting story about a mother cardinal teaching her young their table manners. He said he was often accused of "nature-faking" on account of the story, but he maintained that this actually happened. During watermelon season, he observed that the cardinals he fed loved watermelon seeds, so he made a practice of saving and curing them for his redbirds. Since watermelon seeds are similar to sunflower seeds, the mother cracked each seed, extracted the kernel, and nipped off a small bit for each of her young. While the mother was cracking the seeds, the babies gathered around her and waited impatiently for their turn to be fed. One morning it seemed that one of the youngsters was more impatient than the others and kept rushing forward to get the morsel from his mother's bill. Finally, the mother got tired of his aggression and gave him a sharp peck on the head and drove him out of the circle. It seemed the mother was trying to teach the baby a lesson in patience as well as manners.

Bedichek said he finally quit telling the story because it sounded so preposterous, until a friend of his told him a similar story that involved a cardinal and a House Sparrow. A male cardinal was preparing to feed his young from a piece of hard toast when he turned his back on the baby. While his back was turned, a House Sparrow flew down and stole the toast from the cardinal. The adult cardinal, thinking it was his youngster who had stolen the bread, promptly trounced the baby, not realizing the sparrow was the real culprit.

During the breeding season of 1991, Dr. Fred Gehlbach observed some behavior that he had never seen before in his twenty years of research on cardinals. Here is how the series of events developed. A pair of cardinals built their first nest of the season three feet from the ground in a small red cedar tree. Four young successfully fledged from this nest. Two weeks later, a second nest was started in a deciduous holly, about thirty feet away from the first nest. Four young successfully fledged from this nest about the middle of June. It was this brood that was so interesting to watch.

When the young from the second brood were about one week old, the female parent started construction on a third nest in a plum tree directly in front of Gehlbach's house. (All three nests were within a thirty- to forty-foot radius of the house.) The parents fed the second brood throughout the third incubation period. For about a week after the third brood hatched,

To help sanitize the nest, this parent removes a fecal sac directly from the nestling's vent.

the second set of chicks continued to beg food from the parents on the ground through the shrubbery that surrounded the third nest tree, but the parents ignored them. Gehlbach said that was when the strange behavior began.

Chicks from the second brood started going directly to the nest when they saw the parents feeding their younger siblings. They sat and begged, and the male parent distributed the food he brought to the nest equally between the nestlings and the fledglings. In the midst of all this commotion, one chick from the third brood hopped out of the nest prematurely at the age of eight days and refused to go back. For the next few days this would-be fledgling flapped its wings a lot but never tried to fly. It just hopped around on the limbs near the nest, and both parents fed it every time they fed the three that remained in the nest. By the time this brood fledged, the male parent had finally succeeded in driving away the young of the second brood.

I have witnessed, through the years, countless cardinal families outside my windows—young at different stages of development accompanied by parents. I have seen them develop from wing-fluttering, begging young to independent individuals thirty-eight to forty-five days old and able to forage on their own. I have watched as the youngsters were transformed from helpless creatures with drab brown plumage and dark bills to juvenile birds mottled brown and red. As they matured further, their bills became coral red, and their feathers turned to golden brown or brilliant red, according to their sex. Having cardinals nest near your home provides the rare privilege of observing close at hand such scenes in the bird's life history.

Brood Parasitism

As already pointed out, the cardinal has a number of enemies. Snakes prey on cardinal eggs, and furred enemies include raccoons, fox squirrels, and cats among others that seem to make a habit of eating cardinal eggs and/or young. Among their feathered enemies is a surprising array of species: Sharp-shinned and Cooper's hawks prey on weak individuals; Blue Jays raid cardinal nests and do away with eggs and young; House Wrens sometimes puncture cardinal eggs; Eastern Screech-Owls eat unsuspecting individuals as they feed at dawn and dusk; and Gray Catbirds and House Sparrows are among the most competitive for nesting sites.

Perhaps one of the most unusual enemies of the cardinal is the cowbird, a bird that parasitizes other birds' nests. The female cowbird lays her eggs in the nests of other species and leaves all parental duties to the host species. The cardinal, especially in the central portions of its range, is a fairly common victim of the Brown-headed Cowbird.

Picture this scenario that I often see outside my own windows during nesting season: A young bird flutters its wings in food-begging fashion as it stands before an adult cardinal. The cardinal cracks open a sunflower seed, extracts the nutmeat, and places it in the mouth of the young bird that is obviously not a cardinal.

How do I know it is not a cardinal? In the first place, it has no hint of a crest. Second, its bill is definitely not shaped like a cardinal's. It is a Brown-headed Cowbird fledgling instead. Then why, you may ask, is the cardinal feeding one that is not of its own kind? The answer is, the cardinal parents were victims of *brood parasitism*.

It would be easy to hate the cowbird. It always irritates me when I look out my window and see a cardinal feeding a young Brown-headed Cowbird, because I know exactly what has happened. While the female cardinal was away from her nest, the female cowbird stole in, removed a cardinal egg, laid her similar white egg speckled with brown, and left it for the unsuspecting foster parent to incubate and raise the young as her own.

The cowbird nestling has the advantage of size from the very beginning because cowbird eggs require only eleven to twelve days of incubation and the cardinal's require twelve or more. Add to its advantage of size its aggression. When the foster parents bring food to the nest, it usually outreaches its nest mates and is the first to be fed. As a result, the cowbird grows more rapidly than the cardinal nestlings. Sometimes it crowds out the smaller young cardinals, often trampling them to death

The female cowbird lays her slightly larger egg (upper right egg) in the nest of the cardinal (as well as numerous other species) and leaves all parental responsibilities to the host parent.

or knocking them out of the nest. When this happens, instead of flying to the ground with food for its own young, the parent ignores the outcast nestling and fills the gaping mouth of the foster child that now dominates the nest.

Irritation is the common reaction among those who observe brood parasitism. It seems natural to abhor the parasite and pity the victim. The truth of the matter is that this practice is a highly developed means of survival for the parasitic species and causes no appreciable cost to *most* of the host species. *Most* but not *all*. The cowbird has caused considerable damage to the populations of such endangered species as the Black-capped Vireo, Golden-cheeked Warbler, and Kirtland's Warbler. But that is another story entirely.

The foster parent does have options. It may merely accept the strange object found in its nest whether it is similar to its own eggs or not. (This is usually the case with cardinals.) It can eject the egg, as American Robins do. It may cover the egg or eggs by adding new nesting materials, thus adding new layers to its nest. There is at least one case on record of a cardinal building a two-story nest. The lower floor contained two cowbird eggs. Rarely, the host may attack the unwanted nestling, or it may abandon the nest and build a new one in a different location. But, generally speaking, the urge to brood and feed overcomes all other drives, and the host incubates the egg and rears the cowbird at the expense of the life of at least one of its own young. And so it goes with cardinals in my own backyard.

Oklahoma ornithologist George M. Sutton declared the Northern Cardinal to be the cowbird's perfect "host" in that state. But, according to his observations there from the late 1950s through the late 1970s, he concluded that brood parasitism does not eliminate the cardinal because the cardinal usually succeeds in rearing at least one of its own young for every one, two, or three cowbirds it rears. So even though I may be infuriated when I see a Northern Cardinal feeding a baby cowbird, the status of *Cardinalis cardinalis* remains intact.

That birds spend a good deal of time preening, dusting, oiling, and otherwise caring for their feathers is no surprise: feathers are probably the most important pieces of avian apparatus.

—Jack Page and Eugene S. Morton, *Lords of the Air*

August and September:
Molting and Maintaining Feathers

*B*irds are unique in the animal world in that they develop feathers. No other animal has feathers, and no bird in the world lacks the ability to develop feathers. One of the earliest birds of which we have fossil evidence is the Archaeopteryx. It lived 160 million years ago. The imprints of its feathers in the fine limestone in which it was found show that they were exactly like the feathers of birds of modern times. The feather is an ancient structure indeed.

Feathers serve many purposes. They act as insulators against cold. They protect the bird's skin from sun, rain, and injury. In most species they enable the bird to fly. In some cases they provide protective coloration so that the bird is camouflaged in its environment. In many species, as in cardinals, the color of feathers denotes the bird's sex. Colorful patches of feathers on some birds play an important role in courtship displays and in territorial battles. Birds produce feathers not only in an array of colors, but also in large numbers. The average ranges from close to one thousand feathers on hummingbirds to more than twenty-five thousand on swans. In short, feathers are very important to birds and contribute up to 12 percent of a bird's weight.

Even though feathers are light and look fragile, they are actually quite durable. Ounce for ounce, feathers are among the most durable structures on Earth. One of birds' most time-consuming activities is maintenance behavior—keeping their feathers in prime condition. They have several ways of doing this: bathing (in pools of water, in dew or condensed fog, in rain, in dust, and in sunlight), preening, oiling, and anting. Cardinals engage in all these activities.

First let us consider water bathing. Since bathing functions as a means of keeping the plumage in order and rarely is done just for cleaning purposes, birds need to bathe in winter as well as in summer. If you have a birdbath in your garden, keep fresh

Like children, cardinals seem to enjoy bathing in the spray of lawn sprinklers.

water in it year-round and you will probably see this act often. First the cardinal (or other bird) steps into the container, wades in with both feet to a depth of about one inch, ruffles the feathers all over its body, lowers its head into the water, and raises it abruptly, flipping droplets of water over its back and wings. It may even dip its wings in the water and swish them around. Then it shakes itself all over, much as a dog does to dry itself and rearrange its fur. Sometimes the bird repeats these actions several times before it flies up and out of the water. Since a wet bird cannot fly quickly to safety, it is important to place your birdbath near cover—under a bush or close to a tree with overhanging limbs, for example—so the bird can escape from cats and other predators.

When birdbaths are not available, birds find other places to bathe. Small birds bathe in the shallow edges of ponds and streams, in snowmelt, or in puddles after a rain. During times of drought, birds have been observed bathing in dew or condensed fog that collects on leaves or on grass. During a drought in Tennessee in 1966, observers watched four female and two male cardinals as they bathed on dew-covered leaves in the crowns of sassafras, red maple, and willow trees. Dousing themselves with the refreshing droplets, the birds went through all the motions of a full bath.

Researcher Amelia R. Laskey once observed a cardinal standing on her driveway while a steady rain was falling. She said the bird shook its wings and tail as though bathing in a pool or birdbath. Like children, many birds seem to enjoy bathing in the spray of lawn sprinklers—from robins, cardinals, towhees, and thrashers to hummingbirds. My friend Pam Moes periodically turns on her lawn sprinkler specifically for this purpose during the summer. Barbara Garland happened to be visiting Pam one day and was able to photograph a female cardinal bathing in the spray while it perched on the branch of a tree.

Kenneth Lowe of Yukon, Oklahoma, relates a story of how he discovered that cardinals enjoy this type of shower. He was watering the summer-parched corn in his garden one day, when he noticed a female cardinal clinging to one of the stalks. When he turned off the water, she flew to the ground for a drink. When she didn't fly away, he decided to try something. At the risk of frightening the bird, he adjusted the hose nozzle to spray and pointed it directly at the bird. He said instead of frightening her, this seemed to be exactly what she had wanted all along, and she proceeded to wash herself in the soft spray. Soon the male cardinal flew down for a drink and then turned his attention to Lowe. While the bird stared at him from a distance of fifteen feet, Lowe turned the hose in his direction and gave the crimson male a thorough dousing. The bird returned to the spray four times before flying to a treetop to preen.

Some species of birds bathe in dust. First they make a shallow scrape, peck in the dirt to loosen it, and then roll their bodies in the dirt and toss dust particles over their wings and backs like droplets of water. I have observed House Sparrows dust bathing in a neighbor's flower bed, but I have never seen cardinals do this. Alexander Wetmore reports one instance when sparrows were unable to find dust to bathe in, and settled for a bowl of sugar.

Late in the nineteenth century, Henry Nehrling observed, "During summer, especially in the late afternoon, the cardinals are often seen dusting themselves in the country roads, near Osage orange and Cherokee rose hedges." Although I have no documented proof, I can only imagine that the nature of some parts of their range in the desert Southwest forces cardinals to resort to this type of bathing. Investigators don't know why birds use this dry shampoo method. Some think it improves the alignment of the barbs on the feathers and helps to dislodge parasites. Whatever the reason, it is fascinating to watch.

Have you ever seen a cardinal or other bird emerge from a shady area into full sunlight and suddenly drop to the ground as if injured or ill? I observed one such cardinal as it crouched low with its belly touching the ground, ruffled its crown feathers, opened its tail feathers like a fan, flopped its spread wings to the ground, and tilted its body to one side, all the while panting with its mouth open. With its back to the sun it remained in this awkward position for several minutes. Cardinals have been observed in this position for a full fifteen minutes in one patch of sunshine. Upon seeing such a sight, you may wonder if the bird is dying of heat stroke, but in fact it is simply sunbathing. Many avian species are known to sunbathe in hot weather and in cold.

Like human sun worshipers all over the world, birds, too, enjoy "soaking up some rays." However, unlike humans, whose skin may be harmed by the ultraviolet rays, birds benefit greatly from their moments in the sun. The bird's body and skin absorb the ultraviolet radiation and stimulate vitamin D production. Some think heat and light may cause parasites that have been hiding deep within the feathers to move to places where the bird can more easily remove them by scratching or preening. Sunshine helps dry feathers after a rain shower or a bath, and during molting when the skin is irritated, it provides a source of energy and comfort.

Feathers have a shaft, or quill, that runs through the middle. On each side of the shaft are vanes with thousands of minute interlocking barbs. When these barbs become ruffled or separated, birds must use their bills to zip them back together. This behavior is called *preening,* and it is the most important single act a bird performs in the care and maintenance of its feathers. It is something that must be done every day of a bird's life.

Preening usually follows bathing. You probably have observed it often among the cardinals, jays, and other birds that frequent your yard. First, the cardinal fluffs up all the feathers in the section it is preening. Then it takes each individual feather in its bill and, beginning at the base and moving to the tip, gently bites and strokes it until all the barbs are smoothed and locked back together again. It probes meticulously under the outer feathers to remove dust and parasites. At times a bird must become a contortionist to preen the hard-to-reach parts of its body. For the head and neck feathers that need attention a bird uses its feet to smooth down the feathers.

Barbara Garland said that the one-footed cardinals she observed in her yard had difficulty preening. With one foot missing, they found it hard to balance. She said each bird used its stub to scratch its head.

Most birds have an oil gland called the *uropygial,* or preen, gland. It is located just above the base of the tail. If you have ever plucked and cleaned a domestic chicken, you know what I am describing. It is a yellowish white lump with a nipplelike orifice. This gland secretes a solution that birds use in preening their feathers. In order to reach it, the bird twists its neck until it can touch the gland with its bill. As if dipping a pen in an inkwell, the bird touches the gland with the tip of its bill and transfers the oil to its feathers with rubbing movements. To oil the feathers that cannot be reached with its bill—the head, for example—the bird transfers oil from its bill to its feet and then rubs its head with its feet. The oil helps waterproof the plumage and helps maintain the feathers' insulating properties by keeping them from drying out and becoming brittle. It also helps to keep the bill in good condition. Some authorities believe the oil acts as an antibacterial and fungicidal agent as well.

Cardinals and many other birds have a curious habit called *anting*—placing crushed or live ants among their feathers, rubbing them through their feathers, or allowing them to crawl through their feathers. When the ants are finished, the birds' plumage looks wet. Many authorities believe that birds use the formic acid secreted by ants to help rid their bodies of lice, mites, and other parasites that give them discomfort and to relieve skin irritation during molting. Other researchers suggest that ant secretions may increase the flow of saliva for use in preening, help in removing stale preen oil, or increase feather wear resistance. More than two hundred kinds of birds worldwide practice anting.

Occasionally birds use substitutes in their "anting" behavior. Some observers have noted the following materials that birds use in the same manner as ants: beetles, mealworms, the flesh of lemons, orange juice, coffee, vinegar, beer, cigarette and cigar butts, hot chocolate, soapsuds, mothballs, and sumac berries.

Feathers are simply horny outgrowths of the skin much the same as our fingernails. Blood carries food and oxygen to the feather through the opening at the base of the shaft. Once a feather has reached its full growth, this opening closes, shutting off its supply of life-giving elements. Then the feather becomes a dead structure. It cannot be repaired if it becomes damaged or broken through wear. However, if for any reason a bird loses an entire feather between molts, a new feather begins to form immediately.

As a young bird matures it goes through several different plumage changes before attaining its adult plumage. In the first few days of its life it loses its natal down and puts on juvenal plumage with which it leaves the nest as a fledgling. In the following weeks it sheds those feathers in exchange for a more mature appearance. Thereafter, most adult birds molt, or shed old feathers and replace them with new, at least once a year. Some molt twice or three times yearly. A few species are known to molt four times a year.

Typically, all feathers on a bird's body are replaced after the breeding season. This is when cardinals seem to disappear from our gardens and stop singing. It almost seems as if they do not want us to see or hear them while they molt. I must admit I could sympathize: they do look rather weird while replacing their finery.

In August one year a puzzled friend called to tell me there was a "black-headed cardinal" feeding in his backyard. When I asked him if he was sure it was a cardinal, he said the bird definitely had a cardinal-like beak, and the rest of its body plumage was typically "cardinal." The thing that puzzled him most was that it had no crest. This crestless cardinal was, in fact, a cardinal that was molting. It had lost the feathers on its head, and the dark skin underneath gave it the appearance of indeed being "black-headed."

But this is not the norm. Fortunately, normal molting is a gradual process rather than an instantaneous one, and most birds maintain adequate plumage protection and the power of flight. Usually birds don't lose all the feathers of one area of the body at the same time. If you could examine the skin of a plucked bird you would note the pits, or follicles, from which the feathers grow. They are not distributed evenly over the bird's body, but rather they are grouped into definite areas called feather tracts. The feathers of a particular tract are normally not lost all at once. In songbirds the process takes place in a wave, beginning with the head, face, and throat, and extending backward gradually, with right and left sides at the same stage simultaneously.

Typically, in most flying birds, the flight feathers are shed and replaced one by one in orderly fashion so that flight is still possible even though a few feathers are missing. Usually, the innermost primary feather on each wing is the first to go. As soon as its replacement begins to grow, the one next to it drops out, and so on, until all flight feathers have been replaced. And it is the same way with the rest of the bird's body, tract by tract.

In a few groups of flying birds all flight feathers are lost simultaneously, so that, temporarily, they are incapable of flight. Loons, grebes, swans, geese, and ducks follow this pattern. When this happens they are naturally vulnerable and literally must go into hiding to protect themselves from harm until flight capability is restored.

With adult cardinals molting usually begins after their last brood has hatched, which is about the middle of August where I live in Central Texas. By late September, molting is complete in most birds around my home. In a notebook that I keep near my favorite bird window, I find these entries:

"August 15: Both adult cardinals look really ragged, with dark patches scattered all over their bodies where feathers are missing."

"August 30: Adult male cardinal looks as if his molt is almost complete. Adult female still a little ragged around head and neck; and flight feathers are not fully grown—wings still very short."

"September 10: Adult cardinals look as if molt is complete— both really handsome in their new finery. Mother still feeding one black-billed young. All three at feeder after rain shower."

"September 11: Saw a young male cardinal almost in full adult plumage. Bill almost totally red. Also saw one young that still has an all-black bill." (Bill color change requires about a month.)

Remember, a songbird the size of a cardinal has thousands of feathers that it must preen every day. This causes a terrific drain of energy, and *replacing* that many feathers at least once a year requires great energy output as well. Since feathers are made up entirely of protein and comprise 4 to 12 percent of the bird's weight, any food supplement we supply during their time of molting is put to good use by the birds in our gardens—another reason for providing food and water for cardinals and other birds of our neighborhoods through every season of the year.

Cardinals usually gather together in flocks in fall and winter, staying in areas where food is plentiful.
—Donald and Lillian Stokes, *A Guide to Bird Behavior*

October through December: When Birds of a Feather Flock Together

*O*ne evening in late November, I looked out my favorite bird window and saw a spectacle not soon to be forgotten—ten pairs of cardinals foraging beneath the sunflower feeder in my backyard. It looked as if someone had scattered on my lawn twenty colorful blossoms. Although I shall long remember that scene, it is not unusual at this time of year to see anywhere from four to sixty or more cardinals in a group. This is called *flocking behavior,* and it is common after the end of breeding season when the last of the juveniles become independent. These flocks, containing both juveniles and adults, remain together throughout early winter and don't break up until February and March.

"Birds of a feather flock together," and why not when flocking has advantages? Number one: because a flock has more eyes and ears than one individual bird, protection against predators is more efficient. A bird in a flock is less likely to be surprised by a hawk or an owl than when it is alone. Just go to a woodland edge in fall or winter, imitate the call of an Eastern Screech-Owl, and see what happens. Immediately, a mixed flock of curious birds—usually including several cardinals—comes out of hiding to mob the unwelcome intruder. The enemy, if it were a real owl, might be intimidated by such numbers and move to a different perch, but it seldom leaves its territory when mobbed. Thus we see mobbing used by flocks of small birds to warn predators rather than to repel them.

Number two: a bird in a flock is less likely to overlook sources of food than when it is alone, whether they are sunflower seeds in a backyard, for example, or natural foods that are abundant during winter months. I cannot stress too much the importance of dependable food sources for birds during cold weather. Fat is not only fuel for birds; it also gives them added layers of insulation against the cold. Cardinals are no exception. They, like most resident North American birds, store layers of fat in sequence and thus build up deposits in different parts of their bodies over time. First, they lay down fat in the neck pouch that is located between the breast muscles. Next, fat overlays the abdomen, then forms under the wings, and ultimately encircles many of the internal organs. Thus the cardinal buys time that helps it to survive under severe weather conditions. It can normally carry about three days' worth of reserve fat—enough to get it through an average ice storm or blizzard. If the cardinal cannot find food by the fourth day, it begins to starve, and death follows swiftly.

Number three: the more birds that roost (sleep) together during severely cold weather, the warmer the individuals will be. In much the same manner as people, birds huddle close together to draw warmth from the bodies of other birds and thus are able to survive long, cold winter nights. Just at dusk you may see cardinals flying singly or in small groups to these roosts, which are often in dense evergreen thickets.

In 1832 Thomas Nuttall, the noted botanical explorer and ornithologist, observed a flock in South Carolina: "in severe weather, at sunset, . . . I observed a flock [of cardinals] passing to a roost . . . which continued, in lengthened file, to fly over my head at a considerable height for more than twenty minutes together . . . and, at daybreak, they were seen again to proceed and disperse for subsistence." He was struck by the beauty of the procession as the last rays of the setting sun "flashed upon their brilliant livery."

The number of birds in these winter flocks remains rather constant. Although individuals may separate themselves from the group, generally they are soon replaced by others. Usually the flocks are fairly evenly divided by sex, but the male cardinals may be slightly dominant over the females, especially in feeding situations. Domestic chickens observe a social hierarchy, or "pecking order," among themselves. Dominant chickens peck subordinates in a certain order without fear of retaliation. It is much the same in a flock of cardinals. Bird A pecks B, C, and D; B pecks C and D; C pecks D; and D pecks no one. A is dominant; D is most subordinate.

At first this pecking order may seem to constitute cruel treatment of the subordinates; but actually, it is advantageous for the individuals as well as for the group as a whole. It lends stability to the group and eliminates fighting for food and water. All members know their places, and each is able to obtain the necessities of life.

In any flock of cardinals, or other birds for that matter, birds maintain an almost equal distance between each other. This phenomenon is known as *individual distance*. No matter how large or small the flock or the size of the area they occupy, each bird always seems to manage to preserve a certain amount of space around itself into which no other bird dares to move.

Even though this may be the season of flocking, don't be surprised if you see a single pair of cardinals at your feeder throughout the winter months. Some cardinals choose not to join a flock, but rather to remain on their breeding grounds, as a pair, through the winter. If you are lucky enough to see a flock of these splendid birds, remember that this is normal behavior for this time of year. I cannot think of a winter scene that is more striking than a flock of cardinals perched in a bare winter tree or shrub or a flock silhouetted against the backdrop of an evergreen. At such a time they look like ornaments on a Christmas tree, and we can be glad that "birds of a feather" do, indeed, "flock together."

Life Expectancy

Often when birds forage and nest in our yards, we claim "ownership" of them and consequently feel a certain degree of responsibility for their well-being. We offer them shelter, water, and nourishing food; we may even try to protect them from such predators as neighborhood cats or bird-eating hawks. We wish for them long, healthy lives.

Just how long can cardinals be expected to live? Generally speaking, the smaller the bird, the shorter its life expectancy; the larger the bird, the longer its life expectancy. If a young bird can survive the first year of life, it may be expected to live a surprisingly long time. Barring accidental death, birds live longer than mammals of similar size. During its first year a bird faces incredible hazards and adversities. Nest predation even before hatching, predation while still in the nest, brood parasitism, extreme weather conditions, accidents, diseases, starvation, encounters with enemies both furred and feathered—all are perils faced by birds in the wild. It is surprising that any survive to maturity.

Precise information on the longevity of birds is not easy to procure. Most of the information we have is gathered from bird-banding data. *Banding* is the term used in America for placing aluminum bands on the legs of wild birds in order to trace their times of migration, behavior, flying routes, destinations, local movements, population changes, and length of life. In Great Britain and Europe the practice is called *ringing*.

Life expectancy, the number of years that a species may be expected to live in the wild, varies dramatically from *longevity,* the natural or potential life span of a bird if it is not killed by an accident or disease. Life expectancy is much shorter than longevity because of the incredible number of hazards in a wild bird's life. In Gehlbach's study of cardinals in Central Texas, of the banded adults, an alarming 94 percent were not seen again in a year or less after banding; but their exact ages at banding were not known in most cases. Among the survivors known to live 2 years or more, fifteen males lived an average of 4.3 years (maximum, 10.1 years). Fourteen females lived 3.5 years (maximum, 10.2 years).

In a study by Amelia R. Laskey of 1,135 cardinals whose life span could have been 3 or more years, only thirty (2.6 percent) reached the age of 3 to 6 years. Her oldest female was 4.5 years of age, and two males reached 6 years. She cites from the literature a female that was 10 years of age and a male 13.5 years old. Her report indicates that this older bird was banded in February 1924 and was last seen in November 1936, when he appeared to be very feeble, although he had mated and reared a brood that year. In one study the maximum recorded life span of the Northern Cardinal in the wild is 15 years and 9 months.

Birds in captivity seem to live longer than those who live in natural surroundings. Of course, they are protected from most of the hazards faced by birds in the wild. A captive cardinal, raised as a house pet in Atlanta, Georgia, lived to the ripe old age of 28.5 years. So you see, if we could find a way to protect our favorite redbird in the wild, it has the potential for a very long life.

Through yet another window you will see how the popularity of this flamboyant red bird affects American culture: as state symbol, athletic mascot, and object of art and literature.

PART 2

The Cardinal in American Culture

Purple lilacs nodding in a New England dooryard, the rich scent of yellow jessamine adrift on the southern night, a loon's laughter echoing eerily across a still lake, stout cactus lifting a crown of pale blossoms to the desert sun, rhododendrons aflame in the misty coolness of northwestern slopes, the meadowlark's sweet, wild song flung on the prairie wind, a cardinal's vivid scarlet flashing against forest green . . .

—The 1982 Fifty State Birds and Flowers Mint Set

The Cardinal as Icon

Well-known poets such as Robert Penn Warren, Walt Whitman, Emily Dickinson, and James Whitcomb Riley, as well as uncounted local versifiers affirm the affection Americans hold for their natural surroundings. The writings of Ralph Waldo Emerson, Henry David Thoreau, John Burroughs, Annie Dillard, and Rachel Carson, to name a few—all urge us to see ourselves as a part of nature, not apart from it. Even Tin Pan Alley melodies, folk songs, barbershop ballads, and show tunes reflect America's love for the birds and flowers that embellish our lives with living beauty.

In 1893 the idea of state flowers was born at the World's Columbian Exposition in Chicago when various women's groups decorated each state's exhibits with flowers native to that state. At the fair a women's organization proposed that a national garland of flowers be selected. Each flower was to be chosen by the people of that state and adopted by the state's legislature. Seven years later bird lovers suggested adopting state birds as well.

Soon campaigns were launched nationwide until each state had selected at least one favorite bird as its avian symbol. Some chose two. In all, thirty-two different species have been named as state birds. In some cases a bird was chosen for economic or patriotic reasons, but typically a bird was selected by sheer popularity based on aesthetic reasons. From 1926 through the early 1930s Audubon societies and women's clubs all over the nation fueled the public's interest in this project by holding popular votes, many of them among schoolchildren.

The Northern Cardinal proved to be the favorite bird, being chosen by seven states. Kentucky led the way when the "Kentucky Cardinal" was declared the official state bird by the legislature in 1926. Six other states followed Kentucky's lead in choosing the cardinal. Illinois was second, in 1929, after a poll of the state's schoolchildren in which the cardinal received 39,226 votes. The Eastern Bluebird was the closest contender with 30,306 votes.

Four years later, in 1933, Ohio joined the ranks of cardinal devotees. A decade later North Carolina voted in the cardinal. West Virginia did so in 1949, Virginia followed suit a year later in 1950, and Indiana in 1963 became the seventh state to adopt this crimson beauty as its state bird.

The U.S. Postal Service got into the act when it issued an attractive set of stamps honoring the state birds and flowers of all fifty states in 1982. The stamps were designed by the first father-son team ever to design a U.S. issue, Arthur and Alan Singer of Jericho, New York. The father, Arthur, created the bird designs, and Alan, the flowers.

Out of curiosity I checked the statistics of the ninetieth Christmas Bird Count (the latest available at the time of this writing) to determine the number of cardinals counted in the seven states that have chosen the Northern Cardinal as their official state bird. Keep in mind that each "count area" is a circle with a 15-mile diameter, or roughly 177 square miles. By no means do these numbers reflect the total number of cardinals that reside in each state mentioned.

My unscientific study revealed the following: Out of 54,550 cardinals counted in these seven states, West Virginia was at the bottom of the heap with 2,480 cardinals at thirteen different sites. Kentucky came in sixth, with 2,940 at eleven sites. Next was North Carolina with 4,521 cardinals counted in thirty-two locations. Indiana won the fourth spot when counters tallied 7,997 cardinals. Illinois placed third with 9,737 cardinals at forty-one sites. Virginia came in second with 10,395 of its favorite redbirds found in thirty-eight different count areas. The landslide victory was won by Ohio, where 16,480 cardinals were counted at fifty-four sites.

Love for the cardinal, the most common garden bird of eastern North America, is reflected in more ways than state symbols and U.S. postage stamps. It has also invaded the athletic arenas of our nation. Baseball's St. Louis Cardinals in the National League and the Phoenix Cardinals in the National Football League are two professional athletic teams that have adopted the cardinal as mascot or symbol. Baseball teams in other leagues found the cardinal attractive as well—the Savannah Cardinals of Georgia, the Front Royal Cardinals of Virginia, the Orleans Cardinals of Massachusetts, the Hutchinson Cardinals of Kansas, the Johnson City Cardinals of Tennessee, and the Peoria Cardinals of Peoria, Arizona. Florida and Kentucky each boast teams affiliated with the St. Louis Cardinals—the St. Petersburg Cardinals and the Louisville Redbirds.

The roster of teams choosing other bird names reads like a checklist of North American birds. A survey of two thousand junior and senior colleges of the United States and Canada discloses that seventy-two schools chose the eagle to represent them on the playing field. Various other birds that proved to be among the most popular were blue jays, seahawks, roadrunners, owls, and—you guessed it—cardinals. Of the schools surveyed, twenty-two—seven junior colleges and fifteen senior colleges—have adopted the cardinal as the symbol or mascot for their school's athletic teams.

The stories of how these colleges decided to adopt the bird reveals some interesting anecdotes. In 1884 Wesleyan University in Middletown, Connecticut, voted to discard lavender as the college color in favor of the more striking cardinal red and black. However, shortly after World War I, the red uniforms became maroon because of a careless error by the manufacturers, and maroon remained their color for several years. In 1925 an Alumni Council referendum reestablished cardinal red as "the shade that makes the strongest, most inspiring contrast with black."

About the same time, many students were seeking a name other than "the Methodists" as the designation for Wesleyan athletes. In 1925 the student body named their literature magazine *The Wesleyan Cardinal,* and a color reproduction of the bird was printed on the cover. Finally, Walter Fricke of the class of 1933 bought a baseball jacket with a cardinal on the breast pocket. The students liked the emblem, and since they were tired of newspaper reporters referring to their gridders as "the mysterious ministers from Middletown," they soon decided to designate their athletes the Cardinals.

As early as 1897 a campus-wide publication at State University College in New York was called *The Cardinal.* A comical portrayal of the Plattsburgh Cardinal, symbol of the school, usually is shown wearing sneakers, but when used in connection with the hockey team the cartoonish cardinal switches his footwear to ice skates.

The University of Louisville's athletic symbol and school colors of cardinal and black were chosen sometime after 1913 to honor Kentucky's official state bird. Their athletic teams became known as the Fighting Cardinals sometime after 1921.

Illinois State's athletic squads have been known as the Redbirds since 1923 when then-athletic director Clifford E. "Pop" Horton and *Daily Pantagraph* sports editor Fred Young collaborated to change the nickname from Teachers. When Horton first went to ISU he began calling the teams Cardinals because of the school colors—cardinal red and white. Young, who was ISU's 1910 basketball captain, later changed the name to Redbirds in his newspaper headlines to avoid confusion with the St. Louis Cardinals baseball team.

Catholic University of America, in Washington, D.C., originally named its teams the Red and Black for the school colors. In 1925 a contest supported by the school newspaper determined that the name should be changed to the Cardinals.

At Ball State University in Muncie, Indiana, there was growing discontent in 1927, over the use of the nickname Hoosieroons. This prompted the school newspaper to sponsor a contest to select a new name with a five-dollar gold piece for the prize. Still, no suitable name was chosen, and one week later, coaches Paul "Billy" Williams and Norman Wann were discussing possibilities. Williams, a loyal fan of the St. Louis Cardinals, commented that he liked the cardinal insignia on a sweatshirt worn by National Baseball Hall of Fame's Rogers Hornsby. Later Williams formally submitted the name for consideration. Another student election was held later that month, and the Cardinal was proclaimed the winner by a landslide.

Saginaw Valley State at University Center, Michigan, chose the cardinal symbol by default. A contest sponsored by the student government determined that Voyagers should be the name of their athletic teams. However, students, faculty, and administration were not really satisfied with this name and decided to accept the first runner-up in the contest—Cardinals—since the school's color had always been cardinal red. After that several cardinal logos were used on the campus until 1974 when the school fielded its first football team. A cartoonish Big Red was adopted at that time and used until 1978 when a new stylized version replaced it. The new Big Red is a symbol for both the men's and women's sports activities.

Other schools and colleges that use the nickname are Catonville Community College in Baltimore, Maryland; Henderson County Junior College in Athens, Texas; Hibbing College, Hibbing, Minnesota; Labette Community Junior College in Parsons, Kansas; Mineral Area Junior College in Flat River, Missouri; North Central College, Naperville, Illinois; Lamar University, Beaumont, Texas; St. John Fisher College, Rochester, New York; and Iowa State University of Science and Technology, Ames, Iowa.

Surprisingly, some schools that are located in places where the Northern Cardinal does not occur chose the crimson beauty to represent them—North Idaho College in Coeur d'Alene is one, and Skagit Valley College in Mount Vernon, Washington, has teams called Cardinals and Lady Cardinals. In the survey, no explanation is given about the origin of the nickname for either of these schools other than the clue of their school colors.

In 1892 Stanford University's student body chose cardinal red as the official school color, and soon thereafter sportswriters began calling Stanford teams the Cardinals, even though *Cardinalis cardinalis* does not occur in the part of California where the school is located. The nickname prevailed until 1930, when the university officially adopted the Indian as its mascot. But that symbol was dropped in 1972 when Stanford's Native Americans met with President Richard W. Lyman and suggested that the Indian was not an appropriate symbol. The president and the student senate agreed and reinstated the nickname Cardinals in reference to their school color.

High schools across North America utilize some variation of a cardinal logo on their uniforms or helmets. They are too numerous to list here, testimony that the popularity of this beautiful red bird is very well established all across the land.

If ever there was a Bird of Christmas, it would have to be the male Northern Cardinal.

—George Harrison, *Sports Afield*

The Cardinal at Christmas

On Christmas Day in 1900, twenty-seven intrepid birders in twenty-six locations, mainly around major northeastern cities, strolled through their designated territories and counted the birds they saw in a twenty-four hour period. Thus was born what is now called the Christmas Bird Count, which takes place every year within a two-week period around Christmas.

Since 1900 the annual event has grown from its original twenty-six locations to more than fifteen hundred, stretching from northernmost Canada to Bogotá, Colombia, to Saipan and Southern Guam. And the participants have increased from the original twenty-seven to well over forty-two thousand who travel by foot, in cars, in marsh buggies, on snowshoes, on skis, in motorized boats, in canoes, in helicopters, in airplanes, and in jeeps, utilizing almost every imaginable mode of travel.

All the information from this annual event is gathered, edited, and reported in *American Birds*, a magazine published under the auspices of the National Audubon Society. Apart from its attraction as a social, sporting, and competitive event, the annual count sheds much light on the early winter distribution of the different species of our native birds—their locations and their numbers. As previously stated, ornithologist Terry Root's analysis of Christmas Bird Count data reveals the northward expansion of the Northern Cardinal over the years.

Root's analysis further reveals that the densest concentrations of cardinals in winter occur on the Mississippi River, both in the South and farther north, and also along the Colorado and Guadalupe rivers in southern Texas. Less dense cardinal populations are found in winter along the Ohio, Arkansas, Brazos, and Red rivers.

No matter how the cardinal ranks in its nationwide abundance according to the Christmas Bird Count of any chosen year, I agree with George Harrison's assessment: "If ever there was a Bird of Christmas, it would have to be the male Northern Cardinal." Walk into any Christmas specialty shop and you will find ample evidence of the popularity of this scarlet beauty as a Christmas symbol. Images ranging from cartoon cardinals to lovely portraits of the bird decorate a wide assortment of Christmas paraphernalia.

You see male cardinals on greeting cards, stationery, paper plates, paper napkins and tablecloths, doormats, light switch plates, candles, candle holders, coffee mugs, plates, glasses, Christmas tree ornaments and lights, bookmarks, mailboxes, Christmas jewelry, and the list goes on and on. Cardinals have become an integral part of the way that many people celebrate the holiday season.

Thero North, a friend of mine who lives in Mercer Island, Washington, conducts her own version of the Christmas Bird Count. She calls it the Christmas Card Bird Count. She performs an actual yearly count and reports that of the cards she receives, more each year feature birds, and about one-quarter of those with birds have cardinals on them. Every year I, too, am the recipient of numerous greeting cards decorated with birds. I have never counted them, but I always save a few—mostly the ones with cardinals. The following verse by Oliver Hereford was on one of my all-time favorite Christmas cards, which featured a pair of cardinals on the front. It expresses my feelings exactly:

"I heard a bird sing in the dark of December,
A magical thing and sweet to remember."

Another of my favorite Christmas cards with cardinals contains a verse adapted from a poem by Lord Byron. This one is framed and hangs on my office wall to cheer and inspire throughout the year.

"A light broke in upon my soul. It was the carol of a bird.
It ceased and then it came again, the sweetest song ear ever heard."

Every year beginning about the first of December we hear Christmas carols almost everywhere we go—in shopping centers, on car radios, in doctors' offices, in grocery stores, and in our homes. Carols are a part of the celebration of Christmas. But on December 26 something mysterious happens: the sounds of Christmas cease, and suddenly there is a quietus that lasts until the next December. It is almost like the fall quietus that occurs in the bird world at the end of breeding season when most birds cease to sing.

For example, in my own neighborhood, after the cardinals finish their breeding cycle and begin their fall molt, suddenly there are no more cardinal songs to cheer my days. And then one day, "in the dark of December," when I think the silence will never end, the Bird of Christmas, a male Northern Cardinal, bursts forth in song in the backyard, and my world is no longer deprived of his lovely carols. When I hear the long-awaited "*What cheer-cheer-cheer,*" there is a feeling of continuity, as the brilliant red bird once again constructs his invisible song barrier in anticipation of spring and the promise of new life to come. And the seasons in the life of the cardinal begin all over again.

May the sights and sounds of cardinals, from January through December, be "a light . . . upon your soul" in every season of the year, bringing you assurance of continuity and connectedness with the whole of life. May their beauty live in your heart all year—"the sweetest song ear ever heard."

Bibliography

Adams, Marjorie Valentine. In *The Gift of Birds,* ed. H. F. Robinson, Washington, D.C.: 141–142. National Wildlife Federation, 1979.

Bedichek, Roy. *Adventures with a Texas Naturalist,* 183–184. Austin: University of Texas Press, 1961.

Belting, Natalia M. *The Long-tailed Bear (and Other Indian Legends),* 62–66. New York: Bobbs-Merrill, 1961.

Bent, Arthur Cleveland, and collaborators. *Life Histories of North American Cardinals, Grosbeaks, Buntings, Towhees, Finches, Sparrows, and Allies,* 1–23. U.S. National Museum Bulletin 237. New York: Dover, 1968.

Burroughs, John. *Great Wilderness Days in the Words of John Burroughs,* 63. Waukesha, Wis.: Country Beautiful, 1975.

Choate, Ernest A. *The Dictionary of American Bird Names.* Rev. ed. Harvard, Mass.: Harvard Common Press, 1985.

Conner, Richard N., Mary E. Anderson, and James G. Dickson. "Relationships among Territory Size, Habitat, Song, and Nesting Success of Northern Cardinals." *Auk* 103 (January 1986): 23–31.

Cruickshank, Allen D., and Helen H. *1001 Questions Answered about Birds.* New York: Dover, 1985.

Dennis, John V. *A Complete Guide to Bird Feeding.* New York: Knopf, 1975.

Dixon, Royal. *The Human Side of Birds.* New York: Halcyon House, 1917.

Dow, D. D., and D. M. Scott. "Cardinal Dispersal and Range Expansion." *Canadian Journal of Zoology* 49 (1971): 195–197.

Dunning, John S., with the collaboration of Robert S. Ridgely. *South American Birds: A Photographic Aid to Identification,* 297. Newtown Square, Penn.: Harrowood Books, 1987.

Durant, Mary, and Michael Harwood. *On the Road with John James Audubon.* New York: Dodd, Mead, 1980.

Ehrlich, Paul R., David S. Dobkin, and Darryl Wheye. *The Birder's Handbook: A Field Guide to the Natural History of North American Birds.* New York: Simon & Schuster, 1988.

Franks, Ray. *What's in a Nickname? Exploring the Jungle of College Athletic Mascots.* Amarillo, Tex.: Ray Franks Publishing Ranch, 1982.

"General Notes." *Auk* 91 (April 1974): 418.

"Growth and Age Determination of Nestling Brown-headed Cowbirds." *Wilson Bulletin* 91, no. 3 (September 1979): 464–466.

Harrison, George. "The Cardinal: Big Red." *Sports Afield* (December 1987): 29–30.

James, Ross. *Glen Loates Birds of North America*. Scarborough, Ontario: Prentice-Hall of Canada, 1979.

Johnsgard, Paul A. "Return and Renewal." In *The Wonder of Birds*, 80. Washington, D.C.: National Geographic Society, 1983.

Ladd, Clifton. "Fly-by-Night Parents." *Texas Parks & Wildlife* 49, no. 6 (June 1991): 44–47.

Lemon, Robert E. "The Displays and Call Notes of Cardinals." *Canadian Journal of Zoology* 46 (1968): 141–151.

Lemon, Robert E., and D. M. Scott. "On the Development of Song in Young Cardinals." *Canadian Journal of Zoology* 44 (1966): 192–196.

Lowe, Kenneth. "A Story of Two Special Cardinals." *Bird Watcher's Digest* 1, no. 2 (November/December 1978): 62–64.

Maslowski, Karl. "Share and Share Alike." *WildBird* 5, no. 9 (September 1991): 32–33.

McElroy, Thomas P., Jr. *Habitat Guide to Birding*. New York: Alfred A. Knopf, 1974.

Montroy, A. Sylvia, "Squash, Anyone?" *Bird Watcher's Digest* 3, no. 3 (January/February 1981): 14–17.

Munro, George C. *Hawaii's Birds,* ed. Robert J. Shallenberger. Honolulu: Hawaii Audubon Society, 1978.

Nash, Stephen. "The Songbird Connection." *National Parks* 64, nos. 11–12 (November/December 1990): 23–27.

National Geographic Society. *Field Guide to the Birds of North America*. 2d ed. Washington, D.C.: National Geographic Society, 1987.

Nehrling, Henry. *Our Native Birds of Song and Beauty,* vol. 2, pp. 185–197. Milwaukee: George Brumder, 1896.

"Nest Selection by Brown-headed Cowbirds." *Wilson Bulletin* 91, no. 1 (1979): 118–122.

"Ninetieth Christmas Bird Count." *American Birds* 44, no. 4 (1989).

Nolan, Val, Jr. "Reproductive Success of Birds in Deciduous Scrub Habitat." *Ecology* 44, no. 2 (Spring 1963): 305–313.

Oberholser, Harry C. *The Bird Life of Texas,* edited with distribution maps and additional material by Edgar B. Kincaid, Jr., vol. 2, pp. 853–856. Austin: University of Texas Press, 1974.

Page, Jack, and Eugene S. Morton. *Lords of the Air*. Smithsonian Books, Washington, D.C. Orion Books, New York, 1989.

Pearson, T. Gilbert, editor-in-chief. *Birds of America*, pt. 3, pp. 63–65. Garden City, New York: Garden City Publishing Co., 1917.

Peterson, Roger Tory, and Edward L. Chalif. *A Field Guide to Mexican Birds*. 2d printing with rev. Boston: Houghton Mifflin Company, 1973.

Pettingill, Olin Sewall, Jr. *Ornithology in Laboratory and Field*. Minneapolis, Minn.: Burgess, 1970.

Potter, Eloise F., and Doris C. Hauser. "Relationships of Anting and Sunbathing to Molting in Wild Birds." *Auk* 91 (July 1974): 537–563.

Reilly, Edgar M., and Gorton Carruth. *The Bird Watcher's Diary*. New York: Harper & Row, 1987.

Ritchison, Gary. "The Singing Behavior of Female Northern Cardinals." *The Condor* 88 (1986): 156–159.

———. "Singing of Male Northern Cardinals. *Wilson Bulletin* 100, no. 4 (December 1988): 594–601.

Root, Terry. *Atlas of Wintering North American Birds: An Analysis of Christmas Bird Count Data*, p. 223. Chicago: University of Chicago Press, 1988.

Scheer, George F., ed. *Cherokee Animal Tales*, pp. 62–64. New York: Holiday House, 1968.

Shankle, George Earlie. *State Names, Flags, Seals, Songs, Birds, Flowers, and Other Symbols*. Rev. ed. New York: H. W. Wilson, 1941.

Shearer, Benjamin F., and Barbara S. Shearer. *State Names, Seals, Flags, and Symbols: A Historical Guide*. New York: Greenwood Press, 1987.

Skutch, Alexander. *Parent Birds and Their Young*. Austin: University of Texas Press, 1976.

Stokes, Donald W., and Lillian Q. Stokes. *A Guide to Bird Behavior*, vol. 2, pp. 247–257. Boston: Little, Brown, 1983.

Sutton, George M. *Fifty Common Birds of Oklahoma and the Southern Great Plains*, pp. 86–89. Norman: The University of Oklahoma Press, 1977.

Terres, John K. *The Audubon Society Encyclopedia of North American Birds*. New York: Alfred A. Knopf, 1980.

Torrey, Bradford. "A Bunch of Texas and Arizona Birds." The Texas Collection, vol. 92, no. 549, pp. 96–104. Baylor University Library, Waco, Texas.

Trautman, Milton B. *The Birds of Buckeye Lake, Ohio,* pp. 395–398. Ann Arbor: University of Michigan Press, 1940.

Udvardy, Miklos D. F. *The Audubon Society Field Guide to North American Birds: Western Region,* p. 660. New York: Alfred A. Knopf, 1977.

U.S. Department of the Interior. *The Breeding Bird Survey: Its First Fifteen Years, 1965–1979.* Fish and Wildlife Service, Resource Publication 157. Washington, D.C.: Government Printing Office.

U.S. Postal Service. *The 1982 Fifty State Birds and Flowers Mint Set.* Washington, D.C.: U.S. Government Printing Office, 1983.

Walton, Richard K., and Robert W. Lawson. *Birding by Ear: Eastern/Central.* Boston: Houghton Mifflin, 1989.

Welty, Joel Carl. *The Life of Birds.* New York: Alfred A. Knopf, 1963.

Wetmore, Alexander, and other eminent ornithologists. *Song and Garden Birds of North America.* Washington, D.C.: National Geographic Society, 1964.